a formalist theatre

Other works by the author:

Books:
Happenings
The Art of Time
Futurist Performance

Playscripts:

Photoanalysis
First Signs of Decadence
Three Structuralist Plays
(Double Gothic
Prisoners of the Invisible Kingdom,
Junk/Neon)

Editor:

The New Theatre

Michael
Kirby

a formalist theatre

University of Pennsylvania Press   Philadelphia

Portions of *A Formalist Theatre* previously appeared in:
The Drama Review, Modern Drama, Formations, Intermedia, The Dumb Ox

Copyright © 1987 by the University of Pennsylvania Press

Library of Congress Cataloging-in-Publication Data

Kirby, Michael.
   A formalist theatre.

   Includes index.
   1. Experimental theater.   2. Theater and society.
I. Title.
PN2193.E86K56   1987   306′ .484   87-5839
First paperback printing 1990

ISBN 0-8122-8055-5 (cloth)
ISBN 0-8122-1334-3 (pbk.)

Design: ADRIANNE ONDERDONK DUDDEN

Printed in the United States of America

Probably the largest audience my brother, Ted, played in front of was at the Rye-Harrison high school football game in 1948. (He also acted in the class play, *Ramshackle Inn*, started on the basketball team, was a starting pitcher on the league champion baseball team, and high jumped in track, but those events were not as well-attended as football games.) The crowd at Harrison filled the grandstands and was packed many-deep around the field because this was the traditional rivalry, the last game of the year, and because both teams were good. We had lost two early games; Harrison was undefeated.

At halftime, Harrison led 12-0. In the locker room, Ted, who had never done anything of the kind, gave a short speech to the players. In the last quarter, Harrison, basically a power team, tried a somewhat tricky play. The ball went to the fullback in the single wing—even then the formation seemed old-fashioned—who faked to the tailback, faked to the wingback coming around, and threw to the tailback. The ball never got there. From my position at defensive right end, I had a perfect view of Ted, crashing in at left end, leaping to intercept the pass. Untouched, he ran 40 yards for a touchdown.

With about two minutes left, we still trailed 12-6; Harrison was forced to punt. Our coach called for "Alabama," a play designed to block punts, and it worked. We had the ball near the goal with time running out. Earlier we had run a pass pattern where the two ends—my identical twin and I—went down about 15 yards and crossed. Now, on third down from the Harrison 14-yard line, we went down, faked the cross and broke to the outside. The ball went to Ted in the end zone. The score was tied. Playing the whole game without substitution and on his way to being voted all-league, Ted had scored all of our points: one touchdown on offense and one on defense. The game ended in a 12-12 tie; we felt almost as if we had won.

More than 20 years later, my wife, my brother and I drove to the outdoor swimming pool at Playland in Rye. Ted and I no longer lived in Rye and had not been back for some time. The white-haired man selling admission tickets to the pool recognized us, though. "Which one of you fellows scored those two touchdowns against Harrison?" he asked. "He did," I said. The man let us all in free. There were many, many other things I got—directly and indirectly—from Ted, some of them of immeasurable value. I don't think I was the only one.

contents

introduction

A Formalist Theatre is based primarily on a number of articles written over more than a decade. Most of them appeared in the *Drama Review,* a quarterly journal I edited for fourteen years (fifty-eight issues from 1971 through 1985). Thus, most of the material was not originally conceived as belonging to a book. It reads as though it had been written for a book, however. The approach and style are consistent. The pieces cover a wide range, and yet they complement each other; the arguments converge. Certain ideas, concepts, and theories are treated from different viewpoints in different articles. Of course, the material has been rewritten and new material added. It is not merely an anthology: the whole is much more than the sum of its parts.

Why the title *A Formalist Theatre?* Basically, it is a book of analysis, theory, and description. What is it that makes the analysis, the theory, and the particular theatre that is described formalist?

Let us begin with a definition of "formal." (Beginning with definitions is a basic characteristic of my approach. We should be sure that we are using words in the same way before we get involved in a discussion.) Of the ten definitions of "formal" given in *Webster's New World Dictionary* the most useful here are: "1. of external form or structure, rather than nature or content" and "6. done or made in orderly, regular fashion; methodical." The analysis, theory, and performances described are all formal by these definitions.

A formal approach to analysis means concentrating on "external form" rather than on the content or meaning of a piece. Most theatre is taught and understood in terms of its meaning, its "inner" content. Theatre, in this approach, *is* its meaning. In *A Formalist Theatre,* theatre is approached not as meaning but as experience. The content approach brings theatre toward literature; one "reads" a performance for its meaning, and most, if not all, of the meaning may be obtained as well from reading the script. A formal approach makes clear the difference between theatre as performance and theatre as literature. The experience of reading is quite different from the experience of attending a performance. To a great extent, it is this difference that is being analyzed here as we examine theatre as an activity of the entire sensory organism rather than as an operation almost exclusively of the eyes—in a very limited way—and the mind.

Concentration on theatre as experience allows us to analyze performances that do not have subject matter, something that a content-oriented approach is helpless to deal with and, therefore, rejects. We are not concerned only with content-laden "drama" but with performances—whether or not they are dramatic, whether or not they involve actors and characterization—that are not "about" anything. Dance, spectacle, nightclub acts, and other forms are all considered equally as aspects of theatrical performance.

Every performance has form; not every performance conveys meaning. In dealing with the formal aspects of performance, *A Formalist Theatre* may be thought of as nonsemiotic or even antisemiotic. It attempts to correct the historical attribution of theatrical significance on the basis of meaning and the concurrent denigration of performances that involve little or no meaning.

The goal is to make the study of theatre as objective and systematic as science, to make it as scientific as possible. This means it should be done in an "orderly, regular fashion"—in other words, it should be formal rather than subjective, impressionistic, opinionated, unsystematic, and informal.

What is the orderly, regular method that will be followed here? The basic tool is the analytical continuum, a device for displaying a particular range of possibilities without evaluating them. To see how this tool works, let us try to define theatre itself. What is theatre? What does it include and not include? What are the range and characteristics of its "analytical continuum"?

Theatre does not occur in nature. It is not accidental. It does not just happen. Intent is a necessary and crucial element. People make something that develops and changes in time—a performance—with the intent of having it affect an audience. Eavesdropping and voyeurism are not theatre because the perceived activity is not intended for an audience.

This formulation allows us, among other things, to escape from a theatre version of a very old philosophical question: Is there any sound if a tree falls in the middle of a huge forest and nobody is there to hear it? Is it theatre if a person performs something when alone or if a full rehearsal of a play is conducted without an audience? By our definition, it would be theatre as long as there was the intent to make theatre, to show the performance at some time to an audience.

Allan Kaprow and others, however, do performances without any intention of showing them to an audience. They may be done alone, privately. Other performers may see certain portions. Sometimes there may be accidental spectators. But the performances are intended to be done—to affect the performer—not to be observed. These performances, which may be called "Activities," are not theatre because they do not have the intent to affect an audience. It is not the mere act of performance that makes something theatre; all theatre is performance, but all performance is not theatre.

Thus it is not the qualities and characteristics of the thing we perceive that determine whether or not that thing is theatre. A sunset or a tornado may have certain spectacular qualities that we associate with theatre. The lighting of a street at night may make it look like a stage setting and the passersby like characters in a romantic or mysterious play. There is no intentionality in nature, however, and things may be theatrical—like theatre—without being theatre.

Nor does an assembled audience make an event theatre. Crowds often gather at the site of an accident or to watch a building burn. Although audience psychology is an important aspect of theatre and may be studied in any audience, the mere presence of an audience does not convert something done without intentionality into theatre.

The intent must be specific, however—the intent to make something that will affect an audience. Many activities are done intentionally, and they gather an audience. They may even be made available to spectators or be presented to an audience, but the way the activities are carried out is not related to their affect on the audience, and they are not theatre. The launching of astronauts or of a space shuttle draws a large crowd; people come from thousands of miles away just to see the event. But the launch is not done *for* the spectators. Its procedures and characteristics are determined by other purposes than to affect the audience. Having an affect does not make the launch theatre. Many things in life affect us without having the intention to do so; some theatre, which by our definition must have the intent to affect us, actually does not affect us at all. It is the intent and not the event itself or its impact on us that makes something theatre.

Sporting events certainly affect an audience. They are not merely made available for viewing, like the space launching, but they are actively promoted and presented to the public. Still, they are not theatre.

A different intentionality controls the activity. A game—even though commercial sports draw many more spectators and have a much greater gross income than theatre does in the United States—is not played primarily for its impact on the spectator but to win. This goal, winning, is functionally independent of, and at times may even contradict, spectator interest. A player or team does not try to make the score close, for example, so that the game will be more interesting for the audience. The game is not designed for its effect on the spectator but for the qualities of competition. Its intent is inner-directed rather than outer-directed.

The important point here for the analysis of theatre is to determine how the behavior of the player of the game relates to intent. Football players do not make a tackle or catch a pass in a certain way because of its effect on the spectator; they do it in the most efficient way, to achieve as directly as possible the goal of winning the game. Any effect on the spectators is secondary and indirect. Of course, there are moments—most of them when the game is not actually in progress—when the athlete may perform directly for the audience. A basketball player, for example, steals the ball. There is no defender between him or her and the basket. The player has an easy shot—and, therefore, a wide choice of ways to shoot. In this situation, the player may choose the most spectacular shot for its effect on the audience and not for its effect on the outcome of the game. He or she may make a "slam dunk," leaping high over the basket to fire the ball directly down through the hoop. For a moment, at least, the presentation moves toward theatre. But this is an exception that proves the rule. At least, it illustrates by contrast the qualities of the more common type of performance.

Thus, although the marching bands and baton-twirlers of the half-time display are theatre, the game itself is not, even though both performances are presented to the same audience. The techniques of the musicians and baton-twirlers have been developed and selected for their effect on the spectator. The techniques of the football player—even though they are, perhaps, just as artificial and removed from everyday life—are employed not for their effect on the spectator but for their efficacy in winning the game.

This conceptualization makes it possible to distinguish from theatre yet another kind of presentation for an audience, or at least one that is often done with an audience: the religious ritual or ceremony. Like theatre, religious rituals and ceremonies are outer-directed, but their intent is not to affect an audience but to accomplish a functional purpose in the metaphysical world. A marriage or initiation ceremony changes the spiritual state or condition—but not necessarily the feelings or thoughts—of certain people. A service for the dead changes the spiritual condition of the deceased in some way. A purification ceremony drives away evil spirits. Each religious ritual has a practical effect in the nonphysical world. Such rituals are designed and performed primarily for this end rather than for their effect on any audience that may happen to be present.

Here we see again that it is a psychological factor, intent, and not the objective characteristics of the performance, presentation, or activity that determines what is theatre. The same ritual may be performed with and without metaphysical intent. If the belief that supports the spiritual efficacy is not present—if it fades and disappears as has happened in some cases with shamanism—and yet the ritual continues to be performed for audiences, the presentation becomes theatre. Yet the design and manner of performance of all religious rituals were developed for practical metaphysical reasons. If the intent changes and the ritual is done as theatre with the intent to affect an audience, these elements undoubtedly change in some way. Conversely, ritualized theatre—performance that adopts the objective style of ritual—is not ritual because the intent is different. These are not pedantic distinctions. Because intent may affect the design of the performance and certainly affects the manner in which the performer functions, it is available to the spectator in subtle but perceptible (and significant) ways.

Let us pause for a moment—our analysis is not quite complete—and see what is happening as this definition of theatre is developed. In the first place, a definition is not necessarily hermetic, sealing everything that "fits" within and excluding everything that does not "fit." It is, perhaps, the description of an absolute state or condition, but many things are found to fit the definition to a degree, to some extent. They slip through the intellectual "walls." They relate, but they do not exactly conform.

A second characteristic of a definition is that it sets up an implied contrast. It makes clear those qualities that are contradictory and antithetical. It indicates what it is not or what it could never be. The definition suggests, so to speak, an antidefinition.

Our definition sets up an implied contrast with everyday life. At one pole we have theatre, which is a performance intended to have an effect on an audience, and at the opposite pole we have everyday life, in which we usually do not perform or direct our behavior toward an audience. Between these poles, the conditions or dimensions of theatre may be seen to exist to a greater or lesser degree. The launching of an astronaut is closer to theatre than a spectacular fire because (in the United States, at least) it is made available to an audience. A football game is even closer to theatre because it is actually presented to the public.

Thus definitions are not used here as examples of either/or thinking. A definition and its opposite are seen as endpoints on a continuum or measuring scale that stretches between them. The polar definitions indicate the qualities and characteristics that can be measured on the analytical continuum. Everything falls somewhere on the scale. It may be at one endpoint or the other—completely within a definition or its opposite. Often it lies somewhere in between—nearer one definition than the other. Sometimes it lies at a point halfway between the two definitions and partakes equally of the characteristics of both.

Analytical continua are more adaptable, more precise, more useful—and more lifelike—than hermetic definitions. They will be laid out and employed here whenever possible. For the analyst, the problem is not only to establish the definitions that act as anchor-points on the continuum but to mark out the measuring points on the scale that stretches between them. As on a ruler or yardstick, it is helpful if there are as many more or less precise points as possible at hypothetically "equal" intervals along the entire length of the continuum.

Usually, the most significant points on a continuum are those in the middle, those that are difficult to place, those that clearly partake somewhat of each of the terminal definitions. They probably tell us more about the characteristics and special nature of the scale than do examples that fit obviously and clearly at one end of the continuum or the other.

Let us look at some other public presentations that are not theatre. To separate them from theatre, we will have to make some precise distinctions. Making these distinctions will help us to locate on the analytical continuum its midpoint—the limit of theatre.

Panel discussions and lectures are intended for presentation to an audience, yet they are not considered theatre. Why not? It is not because of the improvised nature of panels and of many lectures. There are several kinds of completely or partially improvised theatre, including commedia dell'arte. In our conceptualization, the distinction is that panel discussions and lectures primarily intend to convey information to the spectators. The word "affect" rather than "effect" was used in our definition of theatre so as to establish this distinction. Theatre seeks not merely an effect—a response—but an affective response, an emotional and ultimately nonintellectual one. ("Bright light," says Webster in defining the word, "*affects* the eyes.") Thus we may distinguish between the teacher, who is not an example of theatre, and the storyteller or stand-up comedian who is, although there may be little, if any, technical and stylistic difference in their manner of presentation.

What do we mean by affect? Pornographic theatre is a useful example. Although it may be an oversimplification to suggest that the purpose of pornography for males is to cause an erection and ejaculation, this formulation makes quite clear that pornographic theatre is concerned primarily with a physiological response. This is one thing we mean by affect—feeling at a sensory, physiological level. The implications of this concept will form a theme running through the book. (Indeed, it will be proposed in dealing with style that a certain physiological response exists in almost all theatre and that almost all theatre attempts to alter our basic affective state.)

Emotions are taken here to be a particular kind of affect. They are those affects that have been labeled by society and tend to be identified by consciousness. Fear, sympathy, suspense, and so on are emotions commonly experienced in theatre. They have a characteristic intellectual component as well as a particular physiological base. They can be seen, however, as specific recognizable points in the larger field of affect, which is less available to consciousness. Affect, then, is a wider and more general term than emotion.

The intention here, it must be emphasized, is not to set up an antagonism or polarity between the intellect and the emotions. Indeed, the opposite is true. There is no question that affect exists in part as a result of intellectual as well as physiological perceptions. If Webster speaks of light affecting the eyes, he also defines affect in its psychological sense as the feeling attached to an idea. Ideas and concepts may also produce affect and emotion. The polarity that *has* been set up is between the intent to convey information (as in lectures) and the intent to create affect, which may be done through information.

At the same time, we could lay out a psychophysical continuum that would indicate the degree to which a presentation was intellectual or physiological. A pornographic play would be well toward the physiological end of the scale; a didactic political play would be closer to the lecture, even though its intent, too, was to create affect.

There is no doubt that the functioning of the mind and the functioning of the body are closely related. Indeed, they are interrelated. This is extremely important for the concept of affect. Yet the creation of affect through ideas and intellectual images is merely the most obvious instance of this interrelationship. For example, the way the intellect functions, completely apart from any specific intellectual content, also creates and determines affect. This will be a fundamental point in my discussion of structuralism in theatre. Structures themselves create affect. Nevertheless, we cannot overlook psychophysical influences moving in the opposite direction: from the body to the mind. The proposition that the way we think is controlled to a greater or lesser extent by the way our total physiology is functioning will underlie all of our discussion of theatre.

Another way to see the distinction between theatre and modes of presenting information such as lectures and panel discussions is in terms of what we could call a technical continuum. Because their intent is primarily to convey information, lectures and panel discussions tend to use the methods and techniques of everyday life. Perhaps the speaker projects his or her voice so as to reach the entire audience. Perhaps he speaks more slowly, more carefully, more precisely. But panel discussions and lectures are, generally, not performed. They are "given." In theatre, the methods and techniques of everyday life are usually altered, if only because the actors deal with each other rather than with the spectator. Thus we may set up a technical continuum involving vocal volume, size of gestures, degree of artificiality, and so on that stretches between theatre and everyday life. Most lectures and panel discussions fall very close to the everyday-life end of the scale. They use little or no technique and are not seen as theatre. Others tend to use artificial techniques—as does, for example, the stereotypical sermon with its stylized gestures and musicalized vocal patterns—and move toward theatre.

This technical continuum measures what is commonly known as theatricality. The traditional Shakespearean actor, who depends heavily on technique, and the realistic actor, who attempts to create, as much as possible, the impression of everyday life, are both examples of theatre, but one is more theatrical than the other, and they fall at different points on the continuum. At some point on the scale, however, a presentation will stop being seen as theatre and will be seen as life, and vice versa.

The information/affect continuum and the technical continuum are independent of each other. Any presentation may be measured on both of them. Complex and artificial technical presentation does not necessarily mean a high degree of affect, nor does the absence of technique mean an absence of emotion. Postmodern dance showed that the movement possibilities of daily life could be used in an affective presentational context. The professor who dresses as William Harvey and delivers his lecture as though he had just discovered the circulation of blood would fall within the limits of theatre on the technical scale although he would remain, one would hope, at the information end of the other continuum. This should not be a problem. That more than one analytical continuum is needed to distinguish theatre from other phenomena merely shows the complexity of theatre. Many more continua will be needed before the analysis of theatre itself approaches completeness.

Finally, it is possible to separate mechanically transmitted theatre such as films and television from the rest of theatre. When I speak of theatre here, I will be referring to so-called "live" theatre rather than its "canned" and broadcast forms. I make this distinction for aesthetic, sociological, and practical reasons. Because, among other things, live theatre has the possibility of responding or adjusting to an audience as well as relating to a particular performance space, its aesthetics as well as its techniques and procedures are quite different. The situation of live theatre—or, as I will say from now on without adding the modifier, theatre—and of films and television within the society is also vastly different, making any sociological generalizations of little value. At almost all levels, the differences between mechanically transmitted and live performances become more important than the similarities. Little can be gained and much lost by discussing them together.

A Formalist Theatre emphasizes the avant-garde. In part, this is because the avant-garde presents us with the greatest diversity of forms, the most "borderline" cases for analysis. It is in the avant-garde that most of the new and problematical examples of theatre are produced. Yet the emphasis is also one of personal interest, as the examples of my own avant-garde productions will show.

A Formalist Theatre is divided into three sections. In Part I, analytical continua are developed and applied to various aspects of theatre: acting, style, structure, and so forth. In the second part, analysis shifts to the social context of theatre, how it functions within the society. Part III is devoted to a particular kind of formalist theatre, an avant-garde theatre that I call Structuralist. An introduction to each part will attempt to explain their general themes and the relationships between the sections. Each of the three parts is relatively independent and self-sufficient. The first two share a common methodology; the first, particularly in its systematic analysis of theatrical structure, leads directly to the third, in which analysis becomes the theory from which Structuralist performance is, at least in my work, developed.

Thus this book is both theatrical analysis and theatrical theory. Webster defines "analysis" as "a separating or breaking up of any whole into its parts so as to find out their nature, proportion, function, relationship, etc." "Theory" is defined as "an idea or mental plan of the way to do something." Thus intellectual analysis involves the creation of a system of ideas by which an existing phenomenon can be "separated" or "broken up" mentally; theory provides an intellectual base for the creation of phenomena. Theatrical analysis examines existing or historical performance; theatrical theory provokes and originates performance.

Since both the analysis and the theory of theatre involve more or less coherent systems of ideas, analysis and theory might be thought to be identical or interchangeable. Analytical systems might be expected to be useful for creating performance; theoretical systems might be supposed to function as well for analysis as they do for creation. In fact, interchangeability exists in only a limited fashion. The criteria for analysis and theory are quite different. Although one would like to think that any ideas could become the basis for some sort of performance, there is no reason to believe that useful analytical theories are equally useful for creation. Theatrical theory might be tremendously stimulating and fruitful—as Antonin Artaud's, for example, has been—without being comprehensive or coherent enough to apply to the analysis of all performance.

Nor can it be claimed that theory and analysis should be interchangeable or that one intellectual system should serve both functions. It is a possibility, however. One may attempt to make any theatrical theory into an analytical system, any analytical system into theatrical theory. One may test the creative applicability of any analytical system by using it to generate performance; one may try to apply any theoretical ideas to the analysis of performances never considered by the theoretician. If one is interested in innovation, more new ideas may come from the suggestions and indications of an analytical system (in which no creative stimulus was intended) than from theatrical theory (in which it was). When theory is "borrowed," the result is usually predictable.

If one is interested in innovative theatre, a possible approach is to develop an analytical system that can later be used as the basis for creating performances. Analysis should be objective and comprehensive. If it is worked out in detail, it should apply to all performance—that which exists and that which does not yet exist. A complete analytical system should indicate possibilities that have not yet been attempted as well as categorizing those that have. It should point the way to the unusual and the unknown in addition to organizing the familiar and the commonplace.

The problem is that many analytical systems are inductive. They reason, as Aristotle did, from particular theatrical facts or known cases to general conclusions. Thus they may be useful in analyzing existing performance, but they offer no lacunae for discovery of the unusual and the not yet known. They reinforce the status quo. They codify tradition and rigidify convention. If turned into theatrical theory and used as a base for creation, these inductive analytical systems only justify more theatre like that which already exists.

A deductive system—one that reasons from a known principle to an unknown one, from the general to the specific, from a premise to a logical conclusion—is one alternative. Another is to use or modify analytical systems set up for other disciplines and other phenomena. In both cases, the result is the same. There is the possibility that the unknown and the uncommon as well as the ordinary will have a place within the system.

That is what is attempted here. An open deductive system is offered both as an analytical tool and as theory. As theory, it is not based upon an idea of what theatre should and should not be. It does not prescribe the kind of theatre it will produce. It could—and one hopes it will—produce several or many new theatres, each with its own unique characteristics. As theory, the analytical system is intended to be provocative and stimulating rather than prescriptive.

formalist
analysis

We have a great heritage in the analysis of dramatic literature, but it is vitally necessary to develop techniques and methods for the analysis of actual presentations. Many continua for the analysis of performance are constructed in this opening part of the book. Its constant focus is on live performance as opposed to and contrasted with dramatic literature. Although some of the concepts developed here may be useful in working with dramatic literature—most of the techniques of structural analysis, for example, may be applied easily to dramatic texts—emphasis is on the spectator rather than the reader. Thus much of the discussion and many of the tools presented here have limited or no application to dramatic literature.

We begin with an analysis of acting itself. Although, as the reference to playscripts by Peter Handke shows, there can be some indication of acting in written texts, the text does not necessarily control or predict the performance. Any script may be interpreted in many ways; the qualities and characteristics of acting can be determined only in the presence of a live presentation. Traditional, literary-oriented approaches have treated the actor as a tool for conveying information. Here, the concern is with the entire range of behavior on stage, whether or not information is involved.

As is made clear in the fourth chapter, the emphasis throughout is on the experience of the spectator. We are not dealing with the way a performance is done—with theatrical technique—but with the perception of the performance. The attempt is to provide something that will be useful not only as philosophy but for the theatre practitioner. Just as literary analysis contributed much to playwriting, performance analysis should contribute to all of the arts of the stage. This is an attempt to examine and analyze the nature of performance itself.

chapter one

acting and not-acting

To act means to feign, to simulate, to represent, to impersonate. As Happenings demonstrated, not all performing is acting. Although acting was sometimes used, the performers in Happenings generally tended to "be" nobody or nothing other than themselves; nor did they represent, or pretend to be in, a time or place different from that of the spectator. They walked, ran, said words, sang, washed dishes, swept, operated machines and stage devices, and so forth, but they did not feign or impersonate.

In most cases, acting and not-acting are relatively easy to recognize and identify. In a performance, we usually know when a person is acting and when not. But there is a scale or continuum of behavior involved, and the differences between acting and not-acting may be small. In such cases categorization may not be easy. Perhaps some would say it is unimportant, but, in fact, it is precisely these borderline cases that can provide insights into acting theory and the nature of the art.

Let us examine acting by tracing the acting/not-acting continuum from one extreme to the other. We will begin at the not-acting end of the scale, where the performer does nothing to feign, simulate, impersonate, and so forth, and move to the opposite position, where behavior of the type that defines acting appears in abundance. Of course, when we speak of "acting" we are referring not to any one style but to all styles. We are not concerned, for example, with the degree of "reality" but with what we can call, for now, the amount of acting.

NOT-ACTING	ACTING

There are numerous performances that do not use acting. Many, but by no means all, dance pieces would fit into this category. Several Far

Eastern theatres make use of stage attendants such as the Kurombo and Kōken of Kabuki. These attendants move props into position and remove them, help with on-stage costume changes, and even serve tea to the actors. Their dress distinguishes them from the actors, and they are not included in the informational structure of the narrative. Even if the spectator ignores them as people, however, they are not invisible. They do not act, and yet they are part of the visual presentation.

As we will see when we get to that point on the continuum, "acting" is active—it refers to feigning, simulation, and so forth that is done by a performer. But representation, simulation, and other qualities that define acting may also be applied to the performer. The way in which a costume creates a "character" is one example.

Let us forsake performance for a moment and consider how the "costume continuum" functions in daily life. If a man wears cowboy boots on the street, as many people do, we do not identify him as a cowboy. If he also wears a wide, tooled-leather belt and even a western hat, we do not see this as a costume, even in a northern city. It is merely a choice of clothing. As more and more items of western clothing—a bandana, chaps, spurs, and so forth—are added, however, we reach the point at which we see either a cowboy or a person dressed as (impersonating) a cowboy. The exact point on the continuum at which this specific identification occurs depends on several factors, the most important of which is place or physical context, and it undoubtedly varies from person to person.

The effect of clothing on stage functions in exactly the same way, but it is more pronounced. A performer wearing only black leotards and western boots might easily be identified as a cowboy. This, of course, indicates the symbolic power of costume in performance. It is important, however, to notice the degree to which the external symbolization is supported and reinforced (or contradicted) by the performer's behavior. If the performer moves (acts) like a cowboy, the identification is made much more readily. If he is merely himself, the identification might not be made at all.

At this stage on our acting/not-acting continuum we are concerned with those performers who do not do anything to reinforce the information or identification. When the performers, like the stage attendants of Kabuki and No, are merely conveyed by their costumes themselves and not embedded, as it were, in matrices of pretended or represented character, situation, place, and time, they can be referred to as being "non-matrixed." As we move toward acting from this extreme not-acting position on the continuum, we come to that condition in which the performer does not act and yet his or her costume represents something or someone. We could call this state a "symbolized matrix."

NOT-ACTING		ACTING
Nonmatrixed	Symbolized Matrix	
Performing		

In *Oedipus, a New Work,* by John Perreault, the "main performer," as Perreault refers to him rather than calling him an actor, limps. If we are aware of the title of the piece and of the story of Oedipus, we might assume that this performer represents Oedipus. He does not pretend to limp, however. A stick has been tied "to his right leg underneath his pants in such a way that he will be forced to limp." When the "main performer" operates a tape recorder, as he does frequently during the presentation, we do not think that this is a representation of Oedipus running a machine. It is a nonmatrixed performer doing something. The lighting of incense and the casting of a reading from the *I Ching* can be seen as a reference to the Delphic Oracle; the three lines of tape that the "main performer" places on the floor so that they converge in the center of the area can be seen as representing the place where, at the intersection of three roads, Oedipus killed his father, and the limp (and the sunglasses that the "main performer" wears throughout the piece) can be considered to stand for aspects of Oedipus. The performer, however, never behaves as if he were anyone other than himself. He never represents elements of character. He merely carries out certain actions.

In a symbolized matrix the referential elements are applied to but not acted by the performer. And just as western boots do not necessarily establish a cowboy, a limp may convey information without establishing a performer as Oedipus. When, as in *Oedipus, a New Work,* the character and place matrices are weak, intermittent, or nonexistent, we see a person, not an actor. As "received" references increase, however, it is difficult to say that the performer is not acting even though he or she is doing nothing that could be defined as acting. In a New York luncheonette before Christmas we might see "a man in a Santa Claus suit" drinking coffee; if exactly the same action were carried out on stage in a setting representing a rustic interior, we might see "Santa Claus drinking coffee in his home at the North Pole." When the matrices are strong, persistent, and reinforce each other, we see an actor, no matter how ordinary the behavior. This condition, the next step closer to true acting on our continuum, we may refer to as "received acting."

NOT-ACTING			ACTING
Nonmatrixed Performing	Symbolized Matrix	Received Acting	

Extras, who do nothing but walk and stand in costume, are seen as "actors." Anyone merely walking across a stage containing a realistic setting might come to represent a person in that place—and, perhaps, time—without doing anything we could distinguish as acting. There is the anecdote of the critic who headed backstage to congratulate a friend and could be seen by the audience as he passed outside the windows of the on-stage house; it was an opportune moment in the story, however, and he was accepted as part of the play.

Nor does the behavior in received acting necessarily need to be simple. Let us imagine a setting representing a bar. In one of the upstage booths, several men play cards throughout the act. Let us say that none of them has lines in the play; they do not react in any way to the characters in the story we are observing. These men do not act. They merely play cards. They may really win and lose money gambling. And yet we also see them as characters, however minor, in the story, and we say that they, too, are acting. We do not distinguish them from the other actors.

If we define acting as something that is done by, rather than something that is done for or to, a performer, we have not yet arrived at true acting on our scale. "Received actor" is only an honorary title. Although the performer seems to be acting, he or she actually is not. Nonmatrixed performing, symbolized matrix, and received acting are stages on the continuum from not-acting to acting. The amount of simulation, representation, impersonation, and so forth has increased as we have moved along the scale, but, so far, none of this was created by the performer in a special way we could designate as "acting."

Although acting in its most complete form offers no problem of definition, our task in constructing a continuum is to designate those transitional areas in which acting begins. What are the simplest characteristics that define acting?

NOT-ACTING				ACTING
Nonmatrixed Performing	Symbolized Matrix	Received Acting	Simple Acting	

They may be either physical or emotional. If the performer does something to simulate, represent, impersonate, and so forth, he or she is acting. It does not matter what style is used or whether the action is part of a complete characterization or informational presentation. No emotion needs to be involved. The definition can depend solely on the character of what is done. (Value judgments, of course, are not involved. Acting is acting whether or not it is done "well" or accurately.) Thus a person who, as in the game of charades, pretends to put on a jacket that does not exist or feigns being ill is acting. Acting can be said to exist in the smallest and simplest action that involves pretense.

Acting also exists in emotional rather than strictly physical terms. Let us say, for example, that we are at a presentation by the Living Theatre of *Paradise Now*. It is that well-known section in which the performers, working individually, walk through the auditorium speaking directly to the spectators. "I'm not allowed to travel without a passport," they say. "I'm not allowed to smoke marijuana!" "I'm not allowed to take my clothes off!" They seem sincere, disturbed, and angry. Are they acting?

The performers are themselves; they are not portraying characters. They are in the theatre, not in some imaginary or represented place. What they say is certainly true. They are not allowed to travel—at least between certain countries—without a passport; the possession of marijuana is against the law. Probably we will all grant that the performers really believe what they are saying—that they really feel these rules and regulations are unjust. Yet they are acting. Acting exists only in their emotional presentation.

At times in real life we meet people who we feel are acting. This does not mean that they are lying, dishonest, living in an unreal world, or necessarily giving a false impression of their character and personality. It means that they seem to be aware of an audience—to be "on stage"— and that they react to this situation by energetically projecting ideas, emotions, and elements of their personality, underlining and theatricalizing it for the sake of the audience. That is what the performers in *Paradise Now* were doing. They were acting their own emotions and beliefs.

Let us phrase this problem in a slightly different way. Public speaking, whether it is extemporaneous or makes use of a script, may involve emotion, but it does not necessarily involve acting. Yet some speakers, while retaining their own characters and remaining sincere, seem to be acting. At what point does acting appear? At the point at which the emotions are "pushed" for the sake of the spectators. This does not mean that the speakers are false or do not believe what they are saying. It merely means that they are selecting and projecting an element of character—emotion—to the audience.

In other words, it does not matter whether an emotion is created to fit an acting situation or whether it is simply amplified. One principle of "method" acting—at least as it is taught in this country—is the use of whatever real feelings and emotions the actor has while playing the role. (Indeed, this became a joke; no matter what unusual or uncomfortable physical urges or psychological needs or problems the actor had, he or she was advised to "use" them.) It may be merely the use and projection of emotion that distinguishes acting from not-acting.

This is an important point. It indicates that acting involves a basic psychic or emotional component; although this component exists in all forms of acting to some degree (except, of course, received acting), it, in itself, is enough to distinguish acting from not-acting. Since this element of acting is mental, a performer may act without moving. This does not mean that, as has been mentioned previously, the motionless person "acts" in a passive and "received" way by having a character, a relationship, a place, and so on imposed on him by the information provided in the presentation. The motionless performer may convey certain attitudes and emotions that are acting even though no physical action is involved.

Further examples of rudimentary acting—as well as examples of not-acting—may be seen in the well-known "mirror" exercise in which two people stand facing each other while one copies or "reflects," like a mirror, the movements of the other. Although this is an exercise used in training actors, acting itself is not necessarily involved. The movements of the first person, and therefore those of the second, might not represent or pretend. Each might merely raise and lower the arms or turn their head. The movements could be completely abstract.

It is here, however, that the perceived relationship between the performer and what is being created can be seen to be crucial in the definition of acting. Even "abstract" movements may be personified and made into a character of sorts through the performer's attitude. If the actor seems to indicate "I am this thing" rather than merely "I am doing these movements," we accept him or her as the "thing": the performer is acting. But we do not accept the "mirror" as acting, even though that character is a "representation" of the first person. He lacks the psychic energy that would turn the abstraction into a personification. If an attitude of "I'm imitating you" is projected, however—if purposeful distortion or "editorializing" appears rather than the neutral attitude of exact copying—the mirror becomes an actor even though the original movements were abstract.

The same exercise may easily involve acting in a more obvious way. The first person, for example, may pretend to shave. The mirror, in copying these feigned actions, becomes an actor now in spite of taking a neutral attitude. (We could call the mirror a "received actor" because, like character and place in our earlier examples, the representation has been "put upon" that person without the inner creative attitude and energy necessary for true acting. The mirror's acting, like that of a marionette, is controlled from the outside.) If the originator in the mirror exercise put on a jacket, he or she would not necessarily be acting; if the originator or the mirror, not having a jacket, pretended to put one on, it would be acting, and so on.

As we have moved along the continuum from not-acting to acting, the amount of representation, personification, and so forth has increased. Now that we have arrived at true acting, we might say that it, too, varies in amount. Small amounts of acting—like those in the examples that have been given—would occupy that part of the scale closest to received acting, and we could move along the continuum to a hypothetical maximum amount of acting. Indeed, the only alternative would seem to be an on-off or all-or-nothing view in which all acting is theoretically (if not qualitatively) equal and undifferentiated.

"Amount" is a difficult word to use in this case, however. Since, especially for Americans, it is easy to assume that more is better, any reference to amount might be taken to indicate relative value or worth. It would be better to speak of "simple" and "complex" acting with the hope that these terms can be accepted as objective and descriptive rather than evaluative. After all, "simple" and "complex" are terms that may be ascribed easily and without implied value judgment to other performance arts such as music and dance. A ballad is relatively simple compared to a symphony; the ordinary fox trot is much less complex than the filmed dances of Fred Astaire. Let us apply the same analysis to acting, remembering that simple acting, such as in the mirror exercise, may be very good, whereas complex acting is not necessarily good and may, indeed, be quite bad.

Complex acting, then, would be the final condition on our acting/not-acting continuum. What do we mean by complex acting? In what ways can acting be simple or complex?

NOT-ACTING				ACTING
Nonmatrixed Performing	Symbolized Matrix	Received Acting	Simple Acting	Complex Acting

The simplest acting is that in which only one element or dimension of acting is used. Emotion, as we have seen, may be the only area in which pretense takes place. Or, as in the mirror exercise, only an action such as putting on a jacket may be simulated. Other acting exercises attempt to isolate various aspects of acting, and they are proof that behavior, which is complex, can be broken down into simple units.

The simple/complex scale also applies to each individual aspect of acting. Emotion may be generalized and unchanging, or it may be specific, modulating and changing frequently within a given period of time. Inexperienced actors, for example, often "play an attitude," "telling" or indicating the single emotion the spectator should have toward the scene or the character rather than the changing feelings of the character. An action may be performed in a simple or a complex way. In the game of charades, for example, we may only indicate that we are putting on a jacket. As long as our team understands what we are doing, the acting is successful. The same action becomes more complex as details such as the resistance of the material, the degree of fit, the weight of the jacket, and so on are acted.

(The word "indicate" that was just used in connection with charades has negative connotations in the technical vocabulary of American method acting. Practitioners of the method cannot accept an element of acting that exists in relative isolation and is not totally integrated by being "justified" and related to other elements. In other styles, however, isolated acting elements are perfectly acceptable and are used, among other things, to focus attention.)

Acting becomes complex as more and more elements are incorporated into the pretense. Let us say that the performer putting on a jacket is part of a scene: the performer may choose to act emotion (fear, let us say), physical characteristics (the person portrayed is old), place (there is a bright sun), and many other elements. Each of these could be performed in isolation, but when they are presented simultaneously or in close proximity to each other the acting becomes complex. In like manner, it is obvious that when speech is added to mime the resultant acting is more complex than the mime alone; the acting involved in a staged reading will, in all likelihood, be less complex than the acting in a fully staged production of the same script; and so forth.

In part, complexity is related to skill and technical ability. Some styles make use of a highly specialized, complex vocabulary. This does not contradict my earlier statement that the acting/not-acting continuum is independent of value judgments. It is not a question of whether a performer can do certain complex acting well but whether he or she can do it at all. Anyone can act; not everyone can act in a complex way.

Yet the analysis of acting according to simple/complex does not necessarily distinguish one style from another, although it could be used to compare styles of acting. Each style has a certain range when measured on a simple/complex scale, and in almost all performances the degree of complexity varies somewhat from moment to moment. It would be impossible to say, for example, that the realistic style of acting is necessarily more complex than the "Grotowski style" of expressionism. Realism, in its most complete and detailed form, would certainly be considered relatively complex. Yet there are many approaches to realism; some—such as those used in many films—ask very little of the actor and would be considered relatively simple. The film actor may do very little; the camera and the physical/informational context do the "acting." A nonrealistic style such as that developed by Jerzy Grotowski, however, can also be extremely complex. In *The Constant Prince*, the acting was very complex. The impression was not one of overacting but of many things taking place simultaneously in the work of a single actor. Frequently, actors will do nothing when another actor is speaking; they will act less so as to help focus the speaker. In Grotowski's staging, this did not happen. During the Prince's long monologues, the other performers did not decrease the complexity of their acting; their bodies were frequently involved in numerous, detailed, small-scale movements. In part, at least, this complexity may be explained by Grotowski's exercises that are designed to develop the ability of the actor to express different, and even contradictory, things with different parts of his body at the same time. Some companies, however, that use what may be recognized as Grotowski style act very simply.

Thus we have arrived at a scale that measures the amount or degree of representation, simulation, impersonation, and so forth in performance behavior. Although the polar states are acting and not-acting, we can follow a continuous increase in the degree of representation from nonmatrixed performing through symbolized matrix, received acting, and simple acting to complex acting.

Belief may exist in either the spectator or the performer, but it does not affect objective classification according to our acting/not-acting scale. Whether an actor feels what he or she is doing to be "real," or a spectator really "believes" what is seen, does not change the classification of the performance; it merely suggests another area or parameter.

Various types and styles of acting are, indeed, seen as more or less realistic, but, except as an indication of style, the word "reality" has little usefulness when applied to acting. From one point of view, all acting is, by definition, "unreal" because pretense, impersonation, and so forth are involved. From another point of view, all acting is real. Philosophically, a No play is as real (if not as realistic) as a Chekhov production. Pretense and impersonation, even in those rare cases when they are not recognized as such, are as real as anything else.

Most plays, of course, even the most naturalistic ones, do not attempt to fool the observer into thinking that they are "real"—that they do not involve acting. Illusionary stagecraft and realistic acting do not intend or expect to be taken for real life any more than an illusionistic painting is intended to be mistaken for what it represents. In almost all performances, we see the "real" person and also that which the actor is representing or pretending. The actor is visible within the character.

To say that no performance can deceive a spectator would not be true, however. True and complete illusion is possible in theatre; acting may actually "lie," be believed, and be seen as not being acting at all. This happened in Norman Taffel's *Little Trips.*

Little Trips began with an enactment by two performers of the story of Cassandra, who was captured by the Greeks when Troy fell. After acting out several incidents—the entry of the Trojan Horse, the rape of Cassandra, among others—the spectators, who were standing around the performing area, were asked to join the actors, if they wished, and to play the same incidents, which would be repeated. At some point in the first or second repetition, while some spectators watched and others participated, the play began to break down. Perhaps one of the spectators protested against spitting in "Cassandra's" mouth, for this was one of the carefully selected images. Perhaps the performers began to argue, and the spectators took sides. At each performance, there was an argument; the play, as it had been described to the spectators in a preliminary introduction, never ended. But this is the way the presentation had been planned. By talking to and exploiting the feelings of the participating spectators, with whom they were able to talk more or less informally, the actors were often able to make them, unknowingly, part of the planned breakdown of the performance. The entire performance was designed to move from the context of art to that of life. Many people actually believed it; indeed, some never discovered that what they thought was a real argument that destroyed the performance had actually been acted.

(During *Little Trips* the two performers changed from a rather simple form of acting that could be more or less copied by participating members of the audience to a conversational style, the realism of which was, perhaps, heightened by the contrast. In terms of our previous discussion of acting, however, it is important to note that the effect of reality did not depend entirely on the acting. It is not only the behavior of the performers but the total performance experience that determines the spectator's response. What creates an illusion in one context will not necessarily do so in another, and in other frames of reference the same acting would have remained "acting.")

There is another type of performance in which the spectator does not recognize the acting for what it really is. An Argentine architect told of her experiences at an all-night religious ceremony on the northern coast of Brazil. At one point, costumed performers appeared who were thought to be dead ancestors. This caused panic among the believers because the doors were locked, and they thought if these ghost-beings touched them they, too, would die. Although belief of this kind obviously affects the quality of the experience, it does not mean that pretense, impersonation, and so forth were not involved in the performance. The appearance of the "dead" ancestors was acted. They knew they were still alive.

Even if the performers believed themselves to be dead, acting would have been involved. Belief would not change the objective fact that something or someone was being represented. This is not to say that belief cannot be an important aspect of acting in certain styles. A principle of the method that achieved the stature of a cliché was the attempt by the actors to believe what the character was doing. If they were successful, the audience would really believe, too. There is no question that this approach has frequently been successful. The attempt to believe undoubtedly attains or approaches with some certainty and predictability the goals that are sought, and it well may be the best approach to these particular problems. At the same time, it is just as clear that belief is not an acceptable criterion for an actor. Many times the actor, when faced with a certain lack of "belief" by the audience, protests that he or she really believed. The important point, however, is that when belief is present or is attained by a performer, acting itself does not disappear. The acting/not-acting scale measures pretense, impersonation, feigning, and so forth; it is independent of either the spectator's or the performer's belief.

Nor can sincerity or commitment be used to define acting. There is the story of the incredibly successful young actor who returns from Hollywood for a visit to his home town. "How do you do it?" his friends ask. "What's the secret?" "There's only one thing you need," the actor answers. "Sincerity." He pauses. "Once you learn how to fake that, you've got it made." As the story indicates, sincerity, too, may be acted. Indeed, the behavior of a person who pretends to be sincere and committed—or underlines theatrically these personality aspects in public presentation—may be seen as another example of simple acting. The story also implies that many people use the appearance of sincerity and commitment as a standard of evaluation. This remains a subjective judgment, however. There is no objective way to measure sincerity and commitment. Nor are these characteristics limited to actors and acting. Everyone—painters, writers, even doctors and teachers—may be sincere about their activities and committed to them. A nonmatrixed performer may be just as committed as someone involved in complex acting.

During the last two decades, theatre in the United States has undergone a more complete and radical change than in any other equivalent period in its history. This is true, at least, of the theatre considered as an art rather than as a craft, business, or entertainment. Since, in the past, almost all of American theatre has been craft, business, or entertainment, this may not be a very startling revelation, but the changes have been striking and extensive. Every aspect of performance has been affected, including acting. As recently as the fall and winter of 1964, the *Tulane Drama Review* devoted two complete issues to Stanislavski; now the method no longer has the absolute dominance it once did in this country, and certain alternative approaches have attracted great interest. Everyone now seems to realize that "acting" does not mean just one thing—the attempt to imitate life in a realistic and detailed fashion.

Thus eclecticism or diversity in the approaches to acting is one aspect of the recent change in American theatre. In terms of our theoretical acting/not-acting continuum, however, we can be more specific: there has, within the last twenty years, been a shift toward the not-acting end of the scale. This means not only that more nonmatrixed performing has been used but that, in a number of ways, acting has grown less complex. A brief review of recent developments will allow us to examine how this has come about while also providing additional examples of the various areas on the acting/not-acting scale.

The most important single factor in the recent changes in performance has been the so-called "Happening." Happenings, of course, are now a part of history. The term is best used in a historical and sociological way to refer to those works created as part of the international Happenings movement of the early and mid-1960s. (The first piece called a Happening was done in 1959, but other generically similar works preceded it, and the term is important only as a reference and as a popular catch-phrase.) The necessary point, however, is that works that, on completely formal grounds, could be called Happenings continue to be done and that almost all of the many innovations produced by Happenings have been applied to narrative, informational, acted theatre. Although I have no wish to perpetuate the name, those who think that Happenings were unimportant, or that the theatre form characterized by Happenings is no longer alive merely because the word is no longer used, do not understand the nature of the form. At any rate, the Happening can help to explain much about current developments in acting.

Under the direct influence of Happenings, among other things, every aspect of theatre in this country has changed: scripts have lost their importance and performances are created collectively; the physical relationship of audience and performance has been altered in many different ways and has been made an inherent part of the piece; audience participation has been investigated; "found" spaces rather than theatres have been used for performance and several different places employed sequentially for the same performance; there has been an increased emphasis on movement and on visual imagery (not to mention a commercialized use of nudity); and so forth. It would be difficult to find any avant-garde performance in this country that did not show the influence of Happenings in one way or another. But Happenings made little use of acting. How, then, could they have anything to do with the recent changes in acting? One way to see their influence is to examine the historical relationship between Happenings and the more prominent United States theatre groups. The history is not very old, but apparent fads are forgotten very quickly.

The last play that the Living Theatre produced before going into its self-imposed exile in Europe was *The Brig*. It was a realistic play with supposed documentary aspects, and it emphasized the "fourth wall"—a high wire-mesh fence closed off the proscenium opening, separating the spectators and the performers. When Le Living opened its next production in Paris in October 1964, the style and form, if not the sociopolitical nature of the content, had changed completely. *Mysteries and Smaller Pieces* was a Happening. (The group would later do another piece, *Paradise Now,* that could also have been called a Happening.)

Of course, *Mysteries* was not called a Happening by the Living Theatre, and few, especially in Europe, recognized it as such. (Claes Oldenburg, who saw the piece in Europe, identified it, but this might be expected. He had seen quite a few Happenings.) At any rate, the performance was without plot, story, or narrative. It was divided into sequential scenes or compartments—one emphasized movement, another sound, another the smell of incense, and so forth. Some even involved acting. The performance was apparently put together on short notice and was the work of the group rather than any one writer. (Almost all of the major Happenings were the product of one artist's imagination, but Happenings often were created by a group, each member of which contributed a specialty—music, design, poetry, and so forth—and the form gained the reputation of being a group creation, thus inspiring those who were dissatisfied with working from an author's previously written script.) Certain images in *Mysteries and Smaller Pieces* came from *The Brig,* but much of it was taken from outside the group and was identical or similar to various Event and Happening images.

In one of the later sections of *Mysteries,* all of the members of the cast died. That is, they pretended to die. Death can be symbolized, but they chose to act it. No acting of this sort was taking place in the Happenings; the Living chose to use elements of acting within the Happening structure. But the acting did not involve character, place, or situation—other than, perhaps, the conditions of the Artaudian plague that was the cause of death. The actors were only themselves, "dying" in the aisles and on the stage of the theatre.

This simplification of acting is typical of much of the work in the new theatre. Indeed, the movement toward the nonmatrixed or reality end of our acting/not-acting continuum made some wonder when death itself would become real rather than being merely acted in performance. In Happening-like presentations, Ralph Ortiz—and others before him— had decapitated live chickens. Peter Brook included the burning of a butterfly in *US.* (Live butterflies were seen flying out of a box, but there is some doubt whether the burned butterfly was indeed real. Cutting the head off a chicken makes death obvious; a butterfly can be faked. "We cannot tell," reads the script of *US,* "if it is real or false.")

One of the scenes in *Mysteries and Smaller Pieces* was a sound-and-movement exercise taken from the Open Theatre. Two lines of performers face each other. A performer from one line moves toward the other line making a particular sound-and-movement combination. A person from the second line "takes" the movement and sound, changing them before passing them on to someone in the first line, and so forth. Like the mirror exercise that was discussed earlier, this use of an acting exercise as an actual performance is one way to simplify acting by concentrating on one or a limited number of elements. Exercises, often more integrated into the action than was this example, were frequently used in the new theatre for their performance qualities and expressiveness rather than for their training values.

This was probably the same exercise that opened the first public performances of the Open Theatre. These presentations, which began in December 1963 and continued into 1965, combined various exercises and short plays on the same bill. It would be foolish to claim a kinship with Happenings for these "variety" programs, but one wonders whether the similarity between the exercises and certain "game" and task-oriented work by, among others, the Judson Dance Theatre did not suggest the possibility of presenting the exercises, which were designed to be done privately, to the public.

Yet another company that showed exercises and made them part of a longer piece is the Performance Group. In its first public presentation, on a 1968 benefit program with other groups, it performed an "Opening Ceremony" composed of exercises adapted from Jerzy Grotowski with certain vocal additions. This "Ceremony" was in *Dionysus in 69* when it opened.

The effect of Happenings on Richard Schechner's work predated the Performance Group, however. The New Orleans Group, which he organized in late 1965, produced a large and spectacular Happening in 1966 and then adapted the various technical means and the audience/performance relationship of the Happening to an "environmental" production of Eugene Ionesco's *Victims of Duty* in 1967. The use of real names, personal anecdotal material, and so forth in *Dionysus in 69* can be seen as an attempt to move away from complex acting toward the non-matrixed performing of Happenings.

Happenings somehow gained the reputation for exhibitionism; some certainly had "camp" aspects. It was probably their use of the untrained performer—the "found" person/actor—that had the most influence on the Theatre of the Ridiculous. John Vacarro, who performed in at least one of Robert Whitman's Happenings, has explained how important the experience was to him. The unabashedly home-made quality of many

Happenings was also an inspiration to many people who did not have an inclination toward slickness, craft, and technique.

This is not to suggest that the general movement toward simplification of acting resulted entirely from the direct influence of Happenings. There have been many factors, all interdependent to some extent: Viola Spolin's improvisations; Grotowski's emphasis on confrontation, disarming, and the *via negativa;* an interest in developing ensembles; the early desire of the Open Theatre to find techniques that were applicable to the Theatre of the Absurd.

Yet influence can also be indirect. Happenings have contributed their share to the creation of a state of mind that values the concrete as opposed to the pretended or simulated and that does not require plots or stories. The most original playwright of recent years, Peter Handke, has worked in this area. Although his plays are quite different from most of the new theatre in this country, many of them illustrate the same concern with simplification of acting.

Offending the Audience and *Self-Accusation* by Handke are unusual plays, if they can be called plays at all. Handke refers to them as "speak-ins" (*Sprechstücke*). They do not employ any matrices of place or character. They take place on plain, bare stages; the actors do not relate to or refer to imaginary locales. The performers are themselves; they are not dressed in any unusual way, nor do they portray characters. In fact, Handke has written dialogue for performers who do not necessarily have to act. The scripts require no pretense or emotion.

The performers speak. They have memorized what Handke has written, and they have rehearsed. But this does not, in itself, make a person an actor. People recite poems and speeches without acting. Musicians rehearse, are concerned with timing, respond to cues. None of these factors defines acting.

What the performers say are, almost entirely, direct statements that would be true no matter who was speaking them. In *Offending the Audience* they speak about the performance situation: "You are sitting in rows. . . . You are looking at us when we speak to you. . . . This is no mirage. . . . The possibilities of the theatre are not exploited here." In *Self-Accusation* the two "speakers," as Handke calls them rather than "actors," talk about themselves: "I came into the world . . . I saw . . . I said my name." There is no need to act to perform this material.

If *Self-Accusation* were played by a blind "speaker," however, the statement "I saw" would be untrue. Or, to take a somewhat less facetious example from the later passages that are no longer so universally applicable, certain people could not say, as if they believed it, the line "I came into the world afflicted with original sin" without feigning. But even a blind person could use the word "saw" metaphorically, and Handke does not suggest that each of the lines has to be given as if the speaker believed it. There are interpretations that would avoid any kind of acting during the performance.

These observations are based only on the script, and there is no script, including Handke's "speak-ins," that can prevent acting. Let us say that a performer creates an emotion. In *Offending the Audience*, for example, the performer pretends to be angry at the spectators when, actually, he is glad they are there. An element of acting has been added to the performance. The presentation would then be using what I have called simple acting. Under a certain director, each of the actors might even create a well-rounded characterization; the acting could become complex. Given the eagerness of actors to act, it is doubtful whether there has ever been a production of these scripts that did, in fact, avoid the use of acting.

Handke's *My Foot, My Tutor* makes use of simple acting by reducing the performers' means: the two characters do not talk, they wear neutral half-masks, and, for the most part, they perform ordinary movements (that sometimes seem extraordinary because they contradict expectancies and do not "fit" the context). The play does involve characters—a Warden and a Ward—but much of the action provokes the question, "What is acted, and what is real?" There is a cat in the play. A cat cannot be trained and does not act. In the performance, "The cat does what it does." Timing depends on the will of the actor, but the length of one scene depends on the length of time it actually takes water to boil in a tea kettle. The Ward eats an apple just as he would if he were not acting, "as if no one were watching." Yet he fails, for no reason, to slice a beet with a large and powerful beet-cutting machine: obviously he is only pretending.

These scripts by Peter Handke show, among other things, that the playwright, too, may use an awareness of the acting/not-acting continuum. Although the playwright's control—exerted only through the written word—over the complexity of acting is limited, he or she may still deal with the nature and degree of acting as an element in the script. And Handke's early work is another illustration of a general, but not universal, shift among contemporary theatre artists toward simple acting and the not-acting end of the scale.

It must be emphasized that the acting/not-acting scale is not intended to establish or suggest values. Objectively, all points on the scale are equally "good." It is only personal taste that prefers complex acting to simple acting or nonmatrixed performing to acting. The various degrees of representation and personification are "colors," so to speak, in the spectrum of human performance; artists may use whichever colors they prefer.

chapter two

the structure of performance

Traditional approaches to structural analysis are primarily inductive. They create rules or principles by generalizing from particular examples— classic Greek tragedies, Shakespeare, the "great" plays. Other forms of theatre are ignored. The emphasis on narrative (and on the script rather than the theatrical production) makes theatrical structure similar to literary structure. Line graphs like those that, at least in cartoons, show the fortunes of Wall Street or the health of a hospital patient are proposed as abstract illustration of theatrical structure. Even when such thinking is relevant to the type of drama from which it is derived, it is useless when applied to other forms of theatre—to dance, variety shows, circus, and so on. Thus all inductive dramatic structural analysis is, at best, incomplete. It may apply to some plays, but it does not consider those aspects of structure that plays share with other forms of theatre.

One approach to establishing a deductive system for the analysis of theatrical structure would be to make the area under consideration as broad as possible and to work, at least in part, from general principles outside the area itself. We are concerned, then, with the structure of theatrical performance, not merely the structure of drama, comedy, ballet, and the like. We may look for principles in sciences such as psychology and in other arts such as kinetic sculpture. We are concerned with any and all principles for analyzing the structure of a phenomenon in time and space.

"Structure" is used to refer to the way the parts of a work relate to each other, how they "fit together" in the mind to form a particular configuration. This fitting together does not happen "out there" in the objective work; it happens in the mind of the spectator. We do not have (or need) equipment such as a microscope or procedures such as chemical analysis to help us understand the structure of theatre. We are not concerned with a mere description or inventory of the elements of a performance but with a study of what the mind does with those elements.

This is subjective. Of course, it may, and probably will, vary from person to person; each person may perceive a somewhat different structure in the same performance. But the same problem has not prevented psychology from attempting to be an objective science. Like the psychologist, we may set down certain general objective structural principles that are concerned with subjective functions.

Structural analysis

If we consider painting as an art to mean the two-dimensional arrangement of line, form, and color, everything that we know about the principles of structure in painting can also be applied to the study of the structure of performance. If we consider sculpture as an art to mean the three-dimensional arrangement of forms in space, everything that we know about the principles of structure in sculpture can also be applied to the study of the structure of performance. Any actors, properties, or scenery on any stage form three-dimensional configurations. If performance analysts were able to deal with the pictorial and sculptural structure of theatre pieces with as much knowledge and in as much detail as art analysts, the study of performance would benefit greatly.

Yet most theatrical structure exists not in the second or third dimensions but in the fourth dimension. The structure of a performance exists primarily in time. Time, the major dimension of performance, can be seen as a sequence of present moments, each of which moves away to become part of the past. This movement is unidirectional. The parts of the continuum have a fixed order and are not interchangeable. It is important to emphasize this characteristic of mental structure as opposed to objective structure. We cannot "reread" a moment in performance. We cannot cut out intervening experience and place a past moment alongside a present one for direct comparison. If we attend a production again and again, we may see relationships that we did not perceive earlier, but that does not change our earlier experience or its structure. Structure "understood" only by rereading or re-viewing does not exist if our concern is only with first-time experience. It is with first-time experience that structural analysis in theatre should be concerned primarily. How the structure of performance changes with repeated viewings may, of course, also be a part of this analysis, but it should always be clear at what level the analysis is made. First-time experience of theatre is the most characteristic and common. If we are concerned with the possible application of analysis as practical theory in the creation of performances, concentration upon first-time structure and the unidirectional flow of experience is particularly important.

Continuity structure: perceptual

Since structure is the way the parts of a work relate to each other, the most significant question in the analysis of performance structure is, "What holds together or unites two moments or parts of a presentation that are separated by time?" To answer this question, let us look first in the most obvious places. When we do, we notice a basic structural principle: anything that exists continuously through time creates structure.

In part, continuity structure exists at the perceptual level. The actor/character is almost always the basic perceptual unit of a play. If an actor is on stage for an extended period, that time duration is held together by the actor's presence. As each present moment fades into the past, there is a common element or factor—the actor—that joins the disparate time experiences. When the actor leaves, the physical continuum ends; that particular structural element is complete.

Thus a play, such as Aeschylus's *Prometheus Bound* or Becque's *La Parisienne*, in which one of the characters is on stage all or almost all of the time, may be seen to be quite different structurally from plays such as Hauptmann's *The Weavers* in which many characters appear and disappear. Claes Oldenburg structured his *Ironworks* and *Fotodeath* by assigning different areas on the stage to different activities. The pieces were then developed by adding and subtracting certain images, none of which physically interacted with the others. The activities merely overlapped each other in time as sometimes two or three, sometimes more, were presented simultaneously. Using this same structure, Robert Wilson built certain of the acts in *The Life and Times of Joseph Stalin* by the addition and removal of characters who "overlapped" but did not interact or play a scene with each other. He "built" an act merely by adding more and more independently functioning characters. Formally, actor/characters may be compared to lines in a drawing or painting. Completely apart from what they represent, their presence holds together and structures the work in a certain way.

The same continuity may be found in the physical aspects of a production. It is obvious, for example, that the following two plays have quite different structures:

ACT ONE *A very large, rather dirty room with whitewashed walls . . .*

ACT TWO   *The same room . . .*
ACT THREE   *The same room . . .*
ACT FOUR   *[The same room] . . .*

(*He Who Gets Slapped* by Andreyev)

and

ACT ONE
  Scene One   *The gate of the castle.*
  Scene Two   *A forest . . .*
  Scene Three   *A hall in the castle.*
  Scene Four   *Before the castle.*

(*Pelléas and Melisande* by Maeterlinck)

Each setting or place holds together or structures the action for a certain amount of time. This does not mean, however, that there is necessarily an absolute physical disjuncture between the scenes of *Pelléas and Melisande*. We would have to analyze particular productions to see how continuing elements—props, costumes, colors, shapes, motifs, lights, and so forth (in addition to actor/characters)—overlap the gaps and fuse the time units at a different level.

This perceptual continuity structure of a performance may be diagrammed by a series of parallel lines of various lengths. Each line would represent the persistence in awareness of a particular physical element; their simultaneity or overlapping as well as their internal continuity would indicate how the performance was held together.

Continuity structure: mental

Psychological continuity—the continuous presence of a mental rather than a physical or perceptual element—also structures segments of extended time. A character/actor, for example, may be present to the mind in various ways even though not on stage and available to the senses. An on-stage character hidden from view (behind a screen, under a bed), a character whose arrival is expected, one who may appear, and one who is talked about also present varying degrees of psychological presence and, therefore, the possibility of a mental continuity structure.

The curtain goes up, revealing activity on a stage; later, the curtain goes down. What occurs between the raising and lowering of the curtain is perceived as a performance. Even when, as in a variety show, the elements of the presentation have no logical or narrative connection with each other, this unification occurs. Structure exists. The "frame" holds together activites in time. When we first consider it, the structure of the rising and falling curtain may be thought to jump across time, connecting two widely separated points and therefore containing everything within. Such jumps across time are a structural possibility, and I will deal with them later, but on a closer examination we find that that is not exactly what happens in this case. When the curtain goes up, something has begun. Each present moment until the curtain falls contains the feeling that something is in progress. Only when the curtain falls does the feeling disappear.

Actions, too, may be continuously present, thus structuring time. Of course, there are actions of various sizes and durations. Some, like the blink of an eye, are so brief that they exist entirely in the present moment, but others, like the search for a murderer, stretch out through time. Most human action is psychophysical; therefore, much of the action of a play has both a psychological and a physical aspect. An eye blink may be merely a startle-response having no mental dimension, but the larger human actions that form the material of most plays involve both motivation and behavior. To the extent that one or the other appears to be dominant, we can talk of "psychological action" and "physical action." Let us say that the intense desire to catch a murderer is manifested by a character, probably through words and gestures, but the actor does do very little physically, performing only a series of small, inconsequential actions. Another character may chase a suspect, fight with him, force a confession from him, and so forth. In the first case, it is more useful to talk of "psychological action," in the second "physical action," although both actions are actually psychophysical. The continuity structure of the former would be mental; that of the latter, perceptual.

An action may be performed by one person or several. All of the characters in a play, therefore, may be taking part in one action. But this large action is made up of many smaller actions. Actions fit "inside" each other like boxes within boxes. Many eyes may blink during the search for the murderer. This means that from one point of view any particular performance is probably structured by the continuity through time of many overlapping actions of various amplitudes and durations.

If smaller, shorter actions—each being a complete entity and having a beginning, middle, and end—are contained within and help to create larger actions, it is the largest action of a performance that is of the most significance structurally. Philosophically it can be claimed that each action/box is within other boxes until life itself becomes the largest all-enclosing box, the supreme action. But no performance can present this action. Structurally we can be concerned only with actions directly presented by the performance, not those which, however logically, may be assumed to exist because of what is given. Because of Hamlet, great political changes take place in Denmark; this larger action is only indicated, however, and its real nature remains a matter of conjecture and imagination.

This does not mean that to be structurally functional, an action has to lie completely within a play. Indeed, the pervasive continuity of an action that began before the curtain rose, went on throughout the performance, and ended, in a manner unknown to the spectator, after the final curtain fell, would hold together the entire presentation. Thus, although Aristotle's emphasis upon a single large action that fills the entire play may seem to be an important structural concept, his requirement that the beginning and end of the action be contained in the performance is merely a question of taste, indicating his persistent attempt to create an ostensibly objective value system that would tell us which plays are good and which are bad.

Momentum; shape

Literary analysis transforms action into a phrase, interpreting and naming it; the action is its description. It seems to function in retrospect, as it were, through reading and rereading the playscript. In actual performance experience, we are conscious of action when we perceive "something going on." We do not have to know *what* is going on. We do not have to wait until the play is over, until the action is complete, to recognize that there is an action or to sense the directionality of that action. From the window of a speeding train, we look out and see a farmer plowing his field. In that instant, we know the action. We know how much he has plowed, his general pattern of progression, and how much he has yet to plow—although, of course, he may never finish the work. Dramatic action may not be as simple to "read," but the same principles apply. Even the momentary awareness of an action of any size implies a past and/or a future, structuring time.

Action contains (is) an energy that flows through time for a particular period. It is by its very nature perceptually or mentally dynamic. It creates expectancy or anticipation of that which has not yet happened. Like the extended arc in Gestalt experiments that is seen as a circle when the missing portion becomes small enough, an action asks the mind to complete it. The energy or force flowing through the present moment moves toward the future. This dynamic energy may be called the "momentum" of an action. Like the current of a flowing river, this momentum may be sampled at single points. The urgency with which the present moment presses toward the future may be measured.

Thus it is not merely a question of whether an action continues in time but of *how* it continues. How much momentum does the action have? Does momentum change or fluctuate? What does each present moment indicate about the past and future of the action?

A dancer—Laura Dean, say, or Andrew de Groat in one of Wilson's productions—is whirling. Steady, uninflected, the whirling continues, passing out of the present moment into the past without change. This we could call the "static mode" of motion perception: the image is essentially unchanging through extended time. It persists, but it gives no indication of "going anywhere."

Steve Paxton in *English*, one of his postmodern dance pieces, is performing a series of poses each taken from and based on a photograph of a person engaged in a sport. The image changes, but the action does not develop. Each moment is dynamically and structurally equal. This could be called the "transitional mode" of perception, in which a series of different present moments flow one into the other without creating operative memories or expectancies.

Most commonly, however, an action changes shape or configuration as it extends through time. (The ways in which the physical continuities of character, setting, costume, and so forth also change and transform have not been mentioned.) If an action exists entirely in the present moment, this shape is received whole and complete. If the action occupies a longer time span, there is the possibility that the whole action will not be registered. In extended actions, memory is necessary to perceive the entire configuration. Expectancy may also be created, predicting the future characteristics of the changing shape from the portion of the action that has already been perceived.

Our diagram showing only a series of straight lines or boxes is no longer adequate as a representation of action structure. We must account for the shape of the action and its momentum. These characteristics may be visualized as a series of plastic shapes of various sizes oriented on the same axis, sometimes partially or completely overlapping each other. Each action shape is made up of many parts—smaller actions that fit together to make the whole. Some of the shapes (the static mode) are rectangular and do not change as they extend through time. Other shapes (the transitional mode) repeat the same configuration over and over. Others (the mode of memory/expectancy) expand, grow narrow, curve, and twist; they have points of varying sharpness, indicating their momentum. Each action shape has a particular duration (length) and relative importance or size (width). Each may be seen; none obscures or hides others.

One characteristic of action is still not represented in this visualization, however. The action shapes imply a passive relationship between action units whose only connection is contiguity. Actually, one action sometimes causes another; there can be a causal chain linking a series or sequence of actions. This is what Aristotle was referring to in the *Poetics* (Chapter X) when he said, "It makes all the difference whether any given event" in the plot, which imitates an action, "is a case of *propter hoc* [because of this] or *post hoc* [after this]." He was calling attention to the difference between actions that caused one another and actions that merely followed or were contiguous to each other.

An action can usually be seen to be composed of other actions arranged in a causal chain. It is—to change the metaphor—like a wave. A wave at one moment is not made up of the same water as that "same" wave of a few seconds later. It is force or energy moving through the water that we identify as a wave. In the same way, energy or force may be seen to move through events that are causally linked, making a larger action. This energy or directional force seems to be the basis for Aristotle's concept of an action that is imitated by a plot. Plot is a causal sequence, and the action flows through it.

Although continuity of action and action momentum are not identical concepts, there is some relationship between them. An action may persist for some time with little or no momentum. No energy is required to form a continuity structure; continuity of high-momentum actions and low-momentum actions both hold together extended time durations. A moment of high-energy action, however, propelling itself into the future, may allow the action to continue and persist in the mind of the spectator even though it is not being represented on stage. It may "jump" across scenes involving other people and actions. Thus durational structures may be divided into two broad categories: continuous and discontinuous. Like ribbons lying in water—their forms and colors fainter when they are below the surface, clearer when they are above—whether persistent elements are considered to be continuous or discontinuous may be a matter of choice. At any rate, their interweaving is a basic characteristic of performance structure.

Discontinuous structure

With the idea of an action jumping "across" intervening unrelated material, we have begun to consider discontinuous structure. Information is usually presented to and assembled by the spectator in a discontinuous fashion. It comes in sudden bursts or "bits," scattered irregularly through the performance like stars in the night sky. Each present moment may contain many bits of information or none at all. Material taken in at one moment and retained in the memory is added to material taken in later. Facts about characters, situations, and actions are built up and assembled. Most plays are a web of information that reinforces, clarifies, and explains itself. This web, holding together many disparate present moments, is the information structure.

At times, information structure tends toward continuity. If certain facts are felt to be needed, the search for them—like a detective looking for clues—may become an active ongoing process creating moment-to-moment continuity. But most frequently information is presented discontinuously. Like a person putting together a picture puzzle, a fact will be fitted in to the information structure by the spectator only when the configuration is correct; if not, it will be discarded, or, more properly, put to one side, until it, too, can be fitted in. These connections are not made at a regular rate. They do not "flow" like an action, even though many of them may refer to and clarify an action. As with the individual parts of a spider's web, connections are made from point to point, as it were, across time.

In part, it is syntax that channels the search for informational connections. Syntax is the rules governing the assemblage of information in verbal communication. In the broadest sense, we can talk about a syntax of performance: the rules governing the assemblage of information from all of the theatrical elements—lights, sound, color, movement, in addition to words. Each of these elements can be used to create signs having meaning, and these meanings add up or combine to form larger meanings—theatrical "sentences," as it were. The operation of syntax involves expectation. If we are given a noun and a particular type of verb, for example, we are led to expect, because of syntax, a direct object. Depending upon the particular noun and verb, we might even be able to predict the exact direct object with some accuracy. This syntactical provocation and channeling of expectation, as well as the making of syntactical connections across time, is structural.

Memory and expectancy are the basis of discontinuous structure. To represent discontinuous structure visually one might use arrows. At each present moment of a performance an arrow to the right, toward the future on the time line of our imaginary chart, would indicate that an expectancy has been created about the future. Perhaps information has been presented that we feel will be useful later. Often, this quality exists even when the performance unit is taken out of context.

DYSART: (shaking hands) Mrs. Strang.
DORA: Mr. Strang's still at the Press, I'm afraid. He should be home in a
minute.
DYSART: He works Sundays as well?
DORA: Oh, yes. He doesn't set much store by Sundays.

(*Equus* by Peter Shaffer [I,7])

If one gets the feeling that this information will be useful, an expectation, which can be represented by an arrow, has been set up. Perhaps, later in the performance, the arrow will reach its target; the syntactic connection will be made. Even if the expectancy is not fulfilled, once it is created it holds together time in a certain way.

Specific memories generated at particular moments in a performance may also be represented by arrows—in this case, arrows pointing back (to the left) along the time line. These connections to the past are not necessarily syntactic. They may not increase in any way the information being conveyed.

Repetition of identical, like, or similar elements is perhaps the basic kind of nonsemiotic discontinuous structure. When a phrase, gesture, or object reappears more than once, it has the tendency to invoke, at some point, the expectation that there will be another. Thus repetition "jumps" in both directions on the time continuum, relating disparate points in an alogical fashion.

Of course, repetition may also relate to meaning and to semiotics. A word or a phrase is often repeated to emphasize and clarify what it means. On the other hand, extreme and rapid repetition tends to destroy meaning; repeated often enough, a word becomes illogical nonsense or pure alogical sound. If one analyzed the experience of listening to a recitation of Tristan Tzara's "Roar" poem—the word "roar" repeated 176 times and the final line, "Who still considers himself quite charming?"— a continuum of meaning/nonsense/sound could probably be plotted. Yet, even though semiotic and nonsemiotic qualities may be considered separately, there is no such thing as completely semiotic repetition. Any semiotic repetition also has a formal dimension. On the other hand, repetition may be completely nonsemiotic, as it is in music.

Most of the structures I have been discussing are purely formal and nonsemiotic. None of them convey meaning in themselves. This does not mean that structure may not have meaning. A structure, too, may become a sign that is joined to a meaning to become a sign-function. *La Ronde* by Arthur Schnitzler, for example, consists of ten scenes, each of two characters. One of the characters in each scene also appears, with a new partner, in the following scene; the new character then reappears in turn. There is no plot, no single action, no overall narrative. The last scene does not contain a new character but one we have met in the first scene—the only character who has not yet reappeared. The progression of characters has come full circle. This unusual patterning in *La Ronde* may be related to meaning, however. The "ring" or "round dance" of the title—and of the structure—may be seen as a metaphor for life.

Structural analysis in painting and sculpture tends to be formal. Theatrical analysis tends to be in terms of meaning and content. Like the painting of a still life, for example, a play may be about something, but the formal aspects of its structure are seldom, if ever, analyzed without reference to its content. The purpose here has been to distinguish between informational (semiotic) and formal (nonsemiotic) structures in performance and to suggest an approach and terminology to deal with the latter, which have been overlooked and neglected.

referential and nonreferential theatre

Some believe that theatre must refer to and make a comment upon the world and everyday life. "What is it about?" they ask on learning of a performance. "What does it mean?" they ask (others and themselves) after having seen it. The assumption is that all theatre must be about something and mean something. Although most theatre—certainly the mainstream of traditional European theatre—is about something and means something, the assumption is not true for all theatre. Let us consider meaning and "aboutness" or reference.

The basic metaphor in referential theatre is the letter or message. Theatre is thought of as one of the mediums through which a message can be sent from the creator to the spectator. In this model, what is most important is not the materials of which the physical message is composed—the ink and paper, so to speak—but the meaning these materials convey. The meaning can be retained and the experience of reading forgotten.

Here we must separate sensory data and information. At the sensory level, we have perceptions of the quality and characteristics of things. No thing has meaning at a purely sensory level. A word, for example, has no meaning as a visual or auditory configuration. Meaning becomes related to things by convention and context. It is ascribed, given, or attached to the sensory units. When this happens, data communicate information about something else—an idea or concept. Thus everything in life provides us with sensory data, but not everything, in these terms, contains or communicates information. Not everything means something.

The connection between sensory data and the information it may communicate is the basic concept of semiotics, the study of how meaning works. We have the sensory configuration and the information it conveys, the sign and its meaning, or, in semiotic terms, the "signifier" and the "signified." Umberto Eco, perhaps the leading semiotician, prefers not to talk of "signs" but of "sign-functions." In this way, he emphasizes that the empirical thing we call the "sign" has no meaning in itself; meaning is joined to it by a code, creating a "sign-function":

> When a code apportions the elements of a conveying system to the elements of a conveyed system, the former becomes the expression of the latter and the latter becomes the content of the former. A sign-function arises when an expression is correlated to a content, both the correlated elements being the functions of such a correlation.   (Umberto Eco, *A Theory of Semiotics*)

Thus we have the basic model of theatre-as-communication. In this model, there is a sender (the creator), a message (the performance) in which meaning is encoded by the sender, and a receiver (the spectator) who decodes—at least to some extent—the meaning. The meaning is the most important thing.

There may appear to be another, more recent, model: that of intuition. Yet the fact that some artists work intuitively and some spectators use intuition in perceiving the work in no way modifies the communication model. Perhaps there are no obvious symbols in the work; form and content may be, so to speak, fused. Even so, if what is put into the work is what is supposed to be taken out, we have the communication model.

In a performance built upon this model, as most performances are, every element is intended to convey meaning or to aid in the process of decoding that meaning. If certain formal qualities are present, that is acceptable, but they, too, are related to, and subservient to, meaning. We could diagram the experience of this kind of theatre as a triangle with meaning at the upper vertex. Figuratively, it rises over all the other elements or aspects of the presentation; all the rest are there only to support the meaning. Or, to modify the metaphor, we might say that the spectator looks through the base of the triangle, through all the material that is the performance, and behind it all is the meaning, which is the most important.

We are still looking through the base of the triangle. At our right and left, the sides of the triangle converge like lines of perspective to meet at a point in the distance. Here we have a metaphor for the way the potentially vast number of particular sign-functions or meaning units are intended, in this model, to converge or come together to communicate one concept or idea—the intellectual theme of the presentation. When a spectator asks, "What does it mean?" it is usually not the individual sign-functions that are in question but the basic theme that, so to speak, brings together, condenses, and concentrates the multitude of small meaning units.

When potential spectators ask, "What is it about?" they might be using the word "about" in either of two ways. They might be asking, "What is the subject matter?" "What are the things that are represented?" Or they might be asking, "What is the theme of the presentation?" "What does it mean?" It is this theatre of thematic meaning, of "about-ness" in the second sense, that I will call "referential theatre." Theatre that does not have a message, contains no intellectual theme, is not "about" life, I will call "nonreferential theatre."

Inefficient decoding and/or "noise" in the system that makes the message difficult to understand are not the only problems encountered by theatre built on the communications model. People often receive messages that were not sent. This is the problem of interpretation. Many supposed messages are projected or read into the reception.

Since the communications model is so old and so commonly used, people often interpret and receive messages from nonreferential works as well. For those who have been brought up to believe that referential theatre is the only possibility and that art must have a message, it is very difficult not to see a message in every work, even ones that are not sending a message. If a message does not appear, the experience is rejected and/or the work denigrated.

Of course, interpretation, too, varies along a continuum. It ranges from a slight misreading of the message to conform to the desires and opinions of the receiver to the often psychotic reception of messages not only from human creations but from natural sources. Antonin Artaud saw tortured figures in the rocks on his journey to the land of the Tarahumaras.

Umberto Eco has dealt with the problem of interpretation by explaining that certain acts of inference "must be recognized as semiotic acts" but only when they are "culturally recognized and systematically coded." This places the emphasis on a culturally established code and distinguishes private, personal, idiosyncratic interpretation from semiotic analysis. Semiotics, then, is not the exegesis of meaning but the demonstration of how meaning derives from a particular code; unless the code itself is clear, we have only interpretation.

The Rorschach test is a perfect example of interpretation and of projection into natural material. To create a test or tool to measure aspects of the personality, Rorschach put ink on pieces of paper and folded the paper, producing symmetrical images. When asked what they see in a Rorschach inkblot, people always see something, although no message has been sent. The inkblot was formed by chance. Rorschach did not claim there was one correct answer, one message, in each blot. All answers are equally correct. The answers tell us something about the person giving them and nothing about the inkblot itself. Yet critics and other people persist in believing that the message they receive is really in the work.

In the inkblot, we have a metaphor for nonreferential theatre. Or we could use the metaphor of a rock, which is a natural object. Like a theatre piece, a rock is a thing, a perceptual object. It has qualities, characteristics, an identity. We experience it. Yet, unless one believes in a God-the-creator who is sending us messages in everything, the rock is not a semiotic object. Like the inkblot and the rock, nonreferential theatre exists for its own sake. It creates an experience without being about something else.

Because we have used a linguistic model to explain referential theatre, it could also be called "linguistic theatre" or "literary theatre." At least since Aristotle's *Poetics,* theatre has been considered to be a branch of literature. Intellectually and academically this approach is still dominant. The written script, of course, *is* literature. It may be studied, analyzed, and discussed just as other literature is: in terms of plot, characterization, imagery, theme, and so forth. Good literature (a good script) is widely believed to be necessary to produce good theatre (a good performance). Inferior literature—many, for example, hold the melodrama to be deficient as literature—is considered unable to produce significant theatre.

Objectively, the literary approach to theatre is as "good" as any other. In any case, since "good" and "bad" are value judgments related to personal taste, there is no use pursuing this particular line of thought. As an analytical approach, however, the examination of the exact ways in which a performance can be considered to be literary will be useful to us. It will help us to distinguish between referential and nonreferential theatre. If those who see theatre as literature like a particular kind of theatre, what are the characteristics of that theatre? How does literary thinking become embodied on the stage? How does it become a part of, or even dominate, the theatrical experience? What is literary threatre?

Some people use the phrase "literary theatre" to designate any performance that is based on a written script; "nonliterary theatre" is any performance that is not derived from a script. This does not necessarily tell us anything about the nature of the presentation. Let us take, for example, an indigenous tribal performance that has been passed on for hundreds of years without ever having a written script. Finally, a script is made up, and performances are derived from it. The new "literary" performances could be identical with the old "nonliterary" ones.

Performance material may be written down and turned into a script at any time before or after the performance. A company, for example, may eschew the playwright, as many have done in recent years, and develop a performance either collectively or under the control of a single director/creator, but the presentation will be the same whether or not it is written down (that is, turned into literature) at some point. Conversely, the fact that anything may be translated into words indicates that a written script may exist for what could be called a "nonliterary" presentation, just as the playing script was finally written down for the tribal performance. When used in this way, the terms "literary" and "nonliterary" merely make a technical distinction. We might as well say "scripted" and "nonscripted" performance.

Our use of the term "literary" is functional and more complex. We are concerned with the qualities of the performance itself and with the spectator's perception of that performance. In our formulation, "literary" means "like literature" rather than "derived from a script." Our hypothesis is that in literary theatre spectators behave in the same way they do when reading literature: they "read" the performance. How, then, do the perceptual mechanisms and the mind work when reading, and what parallels can be seen in theatrical experience?

Although we are focusing on spectator response, we must realize that there is no necessary connection between a work and the way it is perceived in any particular case. Individual responses depend to some extent on the individual. Even when, for example, literary elements exist in a work, literary mechanisms may be "tuned out" or be inoperative for some reason, and the experience may be largely nonliterary. The perception of a Westerner who does not understand Japanese at a performance of No or Kabuki is one example of how, in particular cases, individual experience may be shifted toward the nonliterary. (Since a value system is not involved in this type of analysis, it cannot be said that this experience is "better" or "worse" than that of a spectator who understands Japanese. It is merely different. Indeed, a Westerner might enjoy or like the No more than many Japanese do. Some audiences at No are quite small and contain a high percentage of Westerners.) At any rate, in classifying a work as "literary" we are concerned with the intent to involve certain ways of responding rather than with necessary or universal response.

In reading, the basic action of the mind is that of interpreting signs. The visual or retinal configuration of the written word is translated into meaning. Something that is not there replaces something that is there; the intellectual replaces the physical. Like words, the movements, colors, shapes, sounds, and other elements of a performane may be theatrical signs. The sign process can be seen as the paradigm of literary theatre. In literary theatre, too, the physical and sensory are transformed into the mental.

Although some semioticians have claimed that everything on stage is a sign, this is not true in all cases. The stage attendants of No and Kabuki, the men who manipulate the Bunraku puppets, are not signs. The lights hanging above the stage of a Brechtian production do not signify the sun. A touring theatre troupe is performing on a platform stage in the eighteenth century. We cannot say that the wooden platform or the curtains at the rear are signs. What do the curtains signify in this forest scene, in this scene in Heaven? If the wooden floor signifies earth and clouds in turn, it is not with any great strength or clarity unless it is referred to in the dialogue. And what of the wooden legs of the platform? At what physical point, exactly, does the sign system stop? Here again we have a continuum that stretches from no signification through weak and inferred signification to complete and explicit signification.

Although the sign process is the basis of literary experience, it is important to note that all signs and symbols do not function in the same way. There are different kinds, and, although they can all be considered as literary, some are more literary than others. Words are explicit. Although they may be used in ambiguous ways, their meaning is exact, their definition precise. This is not true of all signs and symbols, however. Some theatrical signs and symbols may be inexact. They may work to some extent in an emotional rather than an intellectual way. They may be suggestive of meaning rather than explicitly communicating it. An allegorical figure such as Death, which is played by a man, in Hugo von Hofmannsthal's *Death and the Fool* or a literal symbol such as the burning candle in Andreyev's *The Life of Man,* which grows shorter and shorter and finally goes out as Man dies, are precise and explicit. Yet what is the meaning of the three old beggars with white hair in Maeterlinck's *Pelleas and Melisande* (II,3) or of the growing castle in August Strindberg's *A Dream Play?* These symbols are more evocative, suggestive, and elusive. It is possible to provide literal meanings, but these meanings seem tentative, partial, or insufficient. The emotion engendered by the image itself—rather than that caused by the meaning of the image—seems to be important.

If we continue in the same direction along this continuum of symbolic explicitness-suggestiveness, we come at the opposite end to those theatrical elements that seem to have the presence or quality of a symbol but lack any specific intellectual content. The second step of the sign process—that of "translation" into meaning—cannot be completed. The elements have the emotional "weight" or "aura" of a symbol but are without its signification. This is what Artaud says he experienced when he saw the Balinese theatre. Because of the cultural differences and his refusal to accept the experience at a purely formal level, he felt the impact of the contentless sign.

Thus, a continuum stretches from those signs and symbols that convey their meaning literally and explicitly, as individual words do, to those "empty" and pseudo-signs that seem to be meaning-carriers but do not impart a meaning. Of course, the clarity of words may be weakened and destroyed by their context. But since words attempt to be precise, the direct relationship to meaning that is found in some signs and symbols may be considered as more literary than those that produce vague, suggested, partial, and emotional meanings. Note that we are not concerned here with multiple meanings. A word, too, may have several meanings. It is the clarity and directness of a theatrical sign that determines its relative literary quality. Yet even the pseudo-sign is literary to a certain extent: it provokes an attempt to "read" the material symbolically, even though the reading cannot provide meaning.

Since it does not involve spoken language, one of the most useful areas in which to construct a sign continuum is that of the silent mime/dancer. At one end of the continuum, the extreme of detailed and explicit symbolization, lies codification such as that of Far Eastern dance-theatre. The hand movements of the *mudras*, for example, are an elaborate gesture language that, like the sign language of the deaf, can represent almost any word. (Although the visual dimension of theatre tends to be less explicit than the verbal, *mudras* indicate that it is pointless to make verbal language the basis for a definition of literary theatre.) Also at this end of the scale are the codifications of stylized French mime with its vocabulary of walking-in-place, door-opening, and so forth. Toward the middle of the continuum are those approaches that, though not codified, attempt to find a gesture language of some sort that will be widely understood and perhaps universal. Much of the emotional expression of modern dance lies in this area: movement signs and sign groups convey "fear," "joy," "longing," and so on. At the suggestive end of the scale are those dancers who work with mood and attitude, who mix sign details into predominantly formal structure, who make only vague reference to visual representation. Finally, at the opposite end of the scale are those dancers who create movement patterns that make no reference to anything else. This kind of movement is nonsign, nonsymbolic, and nonliterary.

Not all performance involves the use of signs. A color, a sound, a figure tumbling through space may be merely a color, a sound, a moving figure. They do not need to indicate anything. They may exist only for their sensory qualities and formal implications rather than for any intellectual component. To the extent that a performance makes use only of elements such as this, it would be purely nonliterary—at least on this first scale or continuum.

A second characteristic of written language—and of literature—is that it involves syntax. In reading, the individual sign units of the words are assembled and ordered into the complex information structures of phrases and sentences. Another mental process, one discussed in the previous chapter, is at work here. We may call it the "syntactical" process. The mind is determining in what ways the basic sign material may be joined so as to increase the intellectual component. A noun relates to a verb or an adjective in particular ways; the combinations produce information of a particular kind. To the extent that this connective mental process is completed as part of the performance experience, the presentation may be seen as literary theatre. To the extent that rules seem to exist for these connections between the sign character of performance elements, we could speak of "theatrical syntax." In grammatical syntax we are concerned with the relationships between word signs; in theatrical syntax we focus on the relationship between the signs of many different kinds that are used in a performance.

Discussing Kabuki theatre in *The Film Form,* Sergei Eisenstein gives an example of what could be seen as theatrical syntax. An actor playing Yuranosuke leaves a castle and moves downstage. The gate behind him is replaced by a smaller painted gate. The small gate and the castle are covered by a curtain that closes in front of them. Samisen music is heard. The actor steps onto the *hanamichi*—the raised walkway that passes through the audience and connects the stage with the rear of the auditorium—and moves toward the rear of the auditorium. A number of theatrical signs—movement, scale change, disappearance, music—all indicate departure from the castle. Each individual sign would not convey the same information by itself, however. The music probably would not have explicit connotation; the change in scale of the gate could indicate that the spectator and not the character was farther away; the curtain could merely denote a scene change; and so forth. When increased meaning is read from a combination of signs, theatrical syntax is functioning.

In the theatrical moment that Eisenstein describes, the actor is the most important element. The other elements are subordinate to him. Even if he did not move, they could convey the stage equivalent of "Yuranosuke leaves the castle," but if he were absent the stage "sentence" would be without a subject.

An adjectival function can be seen in the way colors relate to meaning. Green, for example, has no explicit meaning, although it has a number of diverse associations: sickness, Ireland, "go," envy, money, and so forth. In a particular shape and location, however, it can be limited to any one of its possible implications. It is obvious that theatrical meanings are established by the ways in which a number of signs modify, limit, and qualify each other. It is this theatrical grammar we read when we attend literary theatre.

A sign may be descriptive in its reference. We may imagine, for example, many different stage trees: a mop handle with green paper "branches," two-dimensional drawings of various kinds, a three-dimensional trunk of chicken-wire and painted papier mâché, even a real tree. Each may be seen as a signifier whose signified is "tree." Unlike the word "tree," each tells us something different about what a tree is— each makes a different reference. These different trees, however, may each be seen as a particular and specific collection of signs that, through syntax, conveys a different reference. It is at the level of syntax, and not that of sign, that reference begins.

Just as it is possible to have theatre without signs, it is possible to have a performance without theatrical syntax. In *Hands* by Bruno Corra and F. T. Marinetti, for example, a sequence of twenty images is presented, but none modifies any of the others or increases the meaning derived from them. The images do not "add up." Although there is theatrical structure—an isomorphic structure based on the repeated use of hands—there is no theatrical syntax.

Thus the most significant distinction in art may not be between form and content but between reference and nonreference. Form and content can be separated at the level of the sign-function: the formal signifier is distinct from its signified content. At the level of syntax, however, we may retain the sign and its meaning without making reference. If reference is derived from syntax and not from sign-functions alone, sign-functions may exist in a nonreferential work.

The separation of form and content leads to pure abstraction. Formal perceptual qualities are used rather than ideas and reference. The separation of reference and nonreference, however, leads to what could be thought of as a different kind of abstraction—an abstraction of ideas.

Just as the formal signifier has sensory qualities, an idea may be used for its intellectual "color," so to speak, without making reference. The Happenings, for example, were not completely abstract. They used recognizable symbols and images. Yet they did not make reference. They did not "add up." They did not tell us "about" the things they represented. In the same way, Robert Wilson can use intellectually "colorful" figures such as Freud, Stalin, and Hess without telling us anything about Freud, Stalin, or Hess. Intellectual quality, like sensory quality, can be used for its own sake. If, in referential theatre, all of the elements are arranged in a triangular hierarchy focused on meaning, the same elements may be found in nonreferential theatre, but they will be arranged in a different way.

As in literature, it is the central meaning that is of primary importance in literary theatre. Of course, the governing core of meaning often derives from a script, but it is the meaning and not the script that provides the syntactical focus and makes the presentation literary. Any production that begins from a meaning core—"How can we express or communicate X?"—and elaborates the "message" through any form of theatrical syntax is creating literary theatre.

Since most traditional scripts tell a story, some people confuse literary and narrative theatre. Yet there is no reason that literature has to be narrative. Narrative performance is only one type of literary theatre; nonnarrative forms may also be literary. A common nonnarrative approach, for example, is to pick a theme and develop a number of scenes, images, or skits that relate to it. The Open Theatre did this in *Terminal* and has probably been the greatest influence on this kind of work. If the production attempts to explain or comment on the theme—war, love, race relations, Marilyn Monroe, New York City, the flag, or whatever—the performance will be literary. Yet nonliterary performances may also be built on themes—hands, water, circles, and so forth—without saying anything about these themes, without sending a message to be read from the performance.

Poetry is a form of literature. If we seek its parallel in theatre, we find it not in those poetic dramas whose characters speak in verse but in those performances that are structured like a poem. Like a poem, they make use of syntax, although both poetry and poetic theatre may suspend the rules or work against them at times. Thus, at least in terms of theatrical syntax, the performances of the People Show cannot be considered nonliterary theatre, even though there is no playwright. Like a poem, they are, perhaps momentarily, "about" something. They interweave ideas, images, and symbols much as a nonnarrative poem does. To the extent that meaning is involved, they are literary theatre of a different kind. This is primarily a question of theatrical structure.

A third characteristic of written language is that it controls vision in a very particular and exact way. This is a physiological question rather than a mental one. The eye progresses down the page in an orderly fashion, taking in the sequence of signs and assembling them according to the rules of syntax. Theatrical presentations may be read in an analogous way. In some productions—those that are the most literary—the senses are led in a controlled manner through a sequence of theatrical signs. In other productions—those that are less literary—the reading sequence is not precise or it is nonexistent. To the extent that a reading pattern exists and precise control is exercised over the order in which a spectator perceives theatrical signs, the performance may be said to be literary.

Reading pattern exists to the extent that a spectator's attention is directed first to one theatrical sign and then to another. As in reading literature, theatrical signs in literary theatre are presented singly and in a carefully controlled order. Actors are directed to remain motionless so that the significant gesture will catch the viewer's eye. Stage movement is blocked so that spectators will be looking at a particular place at a particular time. The perceptual pattern is clearly defined; it is expected that every well-meaning spectator will follow it.

Since it is a physiological process, reading pattern can be studied empirically. Apparatus has been developed that uses a small beam of light reflected from the eye to record the eye movements of someone reading or looking at a painting. When the subject looks at a painting, and the recorded tracings of the beam are superimposed on a scaled reproduction of the painting, one can see not only the paths along which the eye moved from one element of the painting to another but those points that received the most attention—the eye came back to them time after time—and those that were ignored. Just as this equipment can compare the way different people "read" or look at a painting, it could compare the way different people read a performance. It could tell us those presentations that had the clearest and most pronounced reading pattern—those in which there was the least variety among the eye movements of the subjects studied.

It is not necessary that theatre make use of reading pattern. Such patterns do not exist in life, and they would not exist, therefore, in absolute stage realism, although they do exist in modified realistic styles. Spectacles such as large dance numbers may be viewed or scanned in many different ways. A stage event may be taken in visually without being "read." Contemplative theatre is not literary; we do not contemplate the printed page. Simultaneity is not literary; we read one word at a time in a set order.

The physical nature of a production does not necessarily indicate anything about the presence or absence of a reading pattern, however. A single sign may be focused in the midst of a large dance number. The reading pattern may call attention to actors in the auditorium as well as those on stage. The deciding factor is the degree to which the spectators' perceptions are implicitly ordered. Rather than reading from word to word, they read from theatrical element to theatrical element.

Note that theatrical reading does not require signs. Since it is the perceptual pattern that is significant, it does not matter whether or not the theatrical elements that are "read" physically are signs and carry meaning. If a performance without signs and syntax moves the spectator's attention from one point to another in sequence, the presentation may be considered to be literary on this particular parameter or continuum.

These three processes—sign-function, syntax, and reading pattern—occur when reading all forms of writing. But it is possible to be even more precise and to point out ways in which the mind works on literature in particular. Webster gives as one definition of "literature," "All writings in prose or verse, especially those of an imaginative or critical character, without regard for their excellence: often distinguished from scientific writing, news reporting, etc." This definition suggests two other mental processes that we may call "literary"—the critical and the imaginative.

Whereas scientific writing and news reporting are not literature because, in their pure state, they deal only with facts about the subject, critical writing involves the mind in making value judgments. These value judgments are not about the work itself, however. They do not indicate whether the play itself is "good" or "bad," whether it is liked or disliked. This spontaneous "criticism" is provoked by every work; we may call it "critical response." Critical writing—and the corresponding form of literary theatre—leads us to make intellectual value judgments about some other thing, idea, or subject. It aims the intellectual evaluative armament at some foreign target, so to speak—the "thing" that referential theatre is "about." To distinguish it from critical response, the mechanism involved may be called "critical reference."

Critical reference asks the spectator to evaluate, weigh, or criticize the subject that the play is "about." Syntactical "aboutness" may exist without critical reference, but the reverse is not true, and critical reference must have a subject. The point of stressing this rather obvious condition is to suggest that theatre that makes critical reference is more literary than that which uses only signs and theatrical syntax.

In his "Preface to Shakespeare," Samuel Johnson found that the Bard, who otherwise might be seen as providing material for strongly literary theatre, was deficient in what we are calling "critical reference." Shakespeare's "first defect," according to Johnson, is that he "is so much more careful to please than to instruct that he seems to write without any moral purpose . . . ; he carries his persons indifferently through right and wrong and at the close dismisses them without further care and leaves their examples to operate by chance." The moral lesson is one form of critical reference.

Political theatre is also a clear example of this mental mechanism. One section of *Mysteries and Smaller Pieces,* a collective creation by the Living Theatre, is the "Dollar Poem" by John Harriman. It involves the recitation of all of the words and numbers found on a United States one-dollar bill. This, in itself, is not political. No value judgments are suggested by the material. No critical reference is inherent in it. But the text is spoken in "loud, clear, bored" voices, and it is juxtaposed with a pantomime of several men cleaning a Marine Corps brig or prison with "military precision." Critical reference is created. We are asked to accept certain value judgments about the dollar, its uses, and the country that produced it. Just as criticism is considered to be a type of literature, this critical reference indicates literary theatre.

The second characteristic of written material that Webster recognizes as particularly literary is the imaginative. This forms our fifth and last dimension or criterion of literary theatre. Like the critical, it can be seen to depend upon a mental process, but the processes are quite different. Imagination is "the act or power of forming mental images of what is not actually present." Words, of course, are the most obvious means for producing imaginative images. (Nouns, for example, would tend to do this, but conjunctions would not, and all words could be placed somewhere on a continuum indicating their relative evocative power.) It is also obvious that certain styles and modes of writing and speaking are designed to produce mental images and that actors in their delivery may enhance this power. A more subtle problem is the extent to which the nonverbal elements of theatre independently produce "mental images of what is not actually present." If, for example, the two-dimensional trees in a Moscow Art Theatre production of Chekhov's *The Seagull* produce mental images of three-dimensional trees, this could be considered a literary aspect of theatre.

If a mime actor propels a nonexistent boat with a nonexistent oar, and we "see" the oar and the boat, imagery is operating. If a man prances across the stage wearing a framework around his hips with a cardboard horse's head mounted on the front, and we see a real horse in our mind, imagery is at work. If dancers (or actors in the new theatre) suggest mental pictures or auditory impressions of birds, serpents, trees, forces of nature, and so forth, imagery is functioning.

Imagery is not hallucination; there is a double nature to its process. We simultaneously experience the mental images and the sensory impressions that caused them. We see that the boat does not exist on stage at the same time that we imagine the boat. The mock horse and the mental image of a horse are perceived in the same moment.

This simultaneity of the mental image process provides one explanation of theatrical reality. In one of his *Lectures* ("Progress of the Drama," 1818), Samuel Taylor Coleridge gave an example of imagery. He and a friend were looking at an engraving "representing a storm at sea without any vessel or boat introduced," when his young son rushed in and saw the print. After a moment of shocked silence, the boy said, "And where is the ship? But that is sunk, and the men are all drowned!" He was imagining something that was not there. The significance of this story is that Coleridge used it to lead into an explanation of theatrical reality: "The true stage illusion . . . consists not in the mind's judging it to be a forest but in its remission of the judgment that it is not a forest." Yet Coleridge did not need to posit "half-faith," "suspension of the act of comparison," and "negative belief." He himself makes the comparison between his theoretical state of stage illusion and dreaming. The point is not merely that all imagery is equal in that "we simply do not judge imagery to be unreal" but that an image has its own reality, which is different from perceptual reality. Since both image and perception—the sunken ship and the print of an empty sea—can exist together, the "reality" of theatre can be in the mind. If mental images are real, and a performance provokes mental images, there is no need to question the reality of the presentation or even to "suspend disbelief" about it.

Imagery does not function equally in all performances. If we see its stimulation as being one standard by which the literary nature of theatre can be judged, our problem is to be able to measure or quantify its occurrence. Imagery is not an either/or function; it can exist at various degrees of intensity and ranges along a continuum stretching from mild suggestion to the state in which mental pictures are more intense than the sensory perceptions of the performance. It is in its weaker forms that it is most difficult to test.

In some theatre, unlike literature, there is often little or no difference between the sign and its mental image. Absolute realism—a tree represented by a real tree, for example—cannot be said to form a mental image of something that is not actually present; the images are of that which *is* present. Mild imagery may be found, however, when realistic staging and acting are not absolutely real. Thus, if both are done realistically, a technically limited amateur production probably will seem more literary than a professional production of the same play because it puts more pressure on the imagination. Simplified or suggestive realism with its generalization, its omission of detail, its truncated arches and indicated walls that substitute the part for the whole, makes direct use of the imaginative process.

This does not mean that the power to provoke imagery is directly related to the degree of abstraction or unreality. Intention is the most important factor; in some nonrealistic performances, it is intended that we imagine nothing. In some performance, the *"isness"* of things is stressed. When we are told somehow that this mop is a tree or that this blue light beam is moonlight, we continue to see only a mop or a beam of light. The mop is used only to convey the idea of a tree rather than its image. The projector with its blue gel is made visible so that its real nature is obvious. Information—a literary element, of course—may be presented, even in nonrealistic forms, without invoking the imaginative process.

Yet if imagery is invoked—and there is no reason why it should be— the difference or distance, so to speak, between the stage image and the evoked image becomes significant. If a mop succeeds in calling up the image of a tree, this indicates greater image power than if a beam of light arouses an image of moonlight. According to this standard, it is the most evocative theatre that is the most literary. After all, literature produces imagery as well as information, and the imaginative response can be seen as important in "reading" a stage performance. It is certainly a contributing factor in the understanding of literary theatre.

Thus, there are four distinct mental mechanisms or processes and one physical process that occur when reading literature. To the extent that these same processes function during a theatrical performance, we may call the performance "literary." The five processes are sign meaning, the syntactical, reading pattern, critical reference, and the imagistic. Each of the five is relatively independent of the others. Theatrical syntax, for example, is not possible without sign meaning, but sign meaning may exist without any of the other qualities. Each, therefore, may be seen to form a continuum of its own, ranging from absence of the particular quality to complete pervasiveness of that quality. When measurements of the five qualities are made, they produce a profile demonstrating the degree to which the performance is literary theatre.

Although they are distinctly different, all of the four mental mechanisms have the common characteristic of using that which is given to the senses as a source for the creation of something else. Those who favor the literary and literary theatre build value systems that emphasize the importance of these mechanisms and their products. Some go so far as to say that theatre cannot exist without them, that the "something else" they produce is vital. Walter Kerr, in *God on the Gymnasium Floor*, explains that the play is really a "third thing" between actor and spectator. It is "intangible," "the thing talked about," "the subject to be discussed." "No play is present," according to Kerr, "when only actors and audience are present" without this "third thing." That is, just as a word is its meaning and not its configuration, a play is its meaning, moral, message, or whatever. (Of course, a word is also a configuration that has a nonliterary effect. This is particularly apparent, for example, to a Westerner, who does not read Japanese, walking at night among the neon signs of Tokyo. And some theatre exists without any literary dimension.) At any rate, Kerr's entirely literary view helps to demonstrate what literary theatre is.

Since each of the five criteria of literary theatre creates an independent continuum and the literary character of the particular performance depends on its combined position on all five of these scales, it can be difficult to compare performances. Both may be literary but in different ways, or each may have a strong literary dimension while remaining relatively nonliterary in the others, and so forth. At any rate, it is important to apply all five criteria when evaluating the literary nature of a performance.

"Literary" and "nonliterary" are of little use as absolute terms. It can be seen that most theatre, including nonverbal forms such as mime and dance, is literary to some extent. Most performance that is predominantly nonliterary has certain literary qualities. "Literary" must mean "relatively or primarily literary." Yet relative terms have their usefulness, too, and it can be important to determine to what extent and in what ways a performance is "literary."

Let us look, for example, at a hypothetical street theatre performance. It has been created collectively by the members of the group, and it has no script, yet it rates as highly literary on each of the five scales. It uses explicit allegorical figures and type characters. Perhaps they even wear signs reading "Uncle Sam," "Doctor," "Unwed Mother," and so forth. A narrative structure is used—let us say that the story is about abortion— and theatrical syntax attempts to make the story clearly understood. The spectator is led carefully from point to point; there is a strong reading pattern. There is a great difference between the stage images and what they represent to the mind—the doctor, for example, is played by a young man in his teens—yet the actors, who speak loudly and make large gestures, want us to think of real people, perhaps people we know. This distance from the real invokes imagery, asking the spectator to imagine something other than what is there. Finally, the play makes a clear and explicit critical reference, asking the spectators to agree with and support pro-abortion legislation. Except for the relatively low density of signs and symbols, this unscripted performance is as literary as any.

We can also—working backward from the five continua—create an imaginary performance that would be toward or at the nonliterary end of each scale. People are moving, dancing, but their movements create no signs; they do not stand for or symbolize anything. Because there are no signs, there can be no syntax. There is no reference to the perceptual world or to an interior world of thoughts, feelings, and emotion. Several dancers are moving at once, and we cannot take in all of the activity at the same time unless we unfocus our vision and contemplate the field as a whole. Or, with focused and directed vision, we may look at first one dancer and then another, our eyes wandering at will, scanning the activity. In neither case has reading pattern been established by the presentation. Because it lacks reference, there is nothing to which value can be ascribed by the performance—there can be no critical reference. Finally, the dancers do not suggest anything but what they are. Imagination is not involved in the spectator's response.

Although this analysis of the literary aspects of theatre is based on the hypothesis that a performance can be "read" by a spectator in much the same way that literature is read, it should be pointed out that the experience of a presentation also may take on literary qualities unrelated to reading. There are ways, for example, in which the awareness of a script may become part of the performance experience. The literary may become a quality of experience through the behavior of the actors. Obviously memorized speech is perceived as a reference to a preexisting text. At these times, the script becomes visible, whereas with a different type of performance, it would not become apparent. Yet it would be deceptive and unnecessary to call this obvious recitation "literary theatre." For one thing, anyone who has listened to inexperienced public speakers and actors knows that a speech may sound "canned" even when it is extemporaneous, and, of course, deliveries based word for word on a literary text may appear completely spontaneous.

The experience of a performance also may indirectly take on a literary dimension. If spectators have read the script of the play they are watching, they may match the presentation with their memory of the written material. They can even bring a book to the performance and read the script as the performers act it out. A literary comparison factor may be one aspect of the total complex response to a staged play. Obviously, this is widely true of classics such as *Hamlet*, but it does not and cannot happen with most performances.

A surrogate experience can take place, however. Once spectators have had the experience of, so to speak, reading the script in their memory at the same time they perceive the actual performance, they may feel that this experience is necessary or important. They may imagine or deduce a mental script from the presentation even when they have not read the actual script. In doing this, they may attribute certain material to the playwright, certain material to the director, and so forth. This mental activity "recreating" a hypothetical written script may also be considered to be literary. A performance, then, could be categorized as literary to the extent that it causes, induces, or supports this activity.

Imaginative recreation of a script is based almost exclusively upon spoken dialogue rather than on stage movement, costumes, scenery, or lighting. The dialogue keeps the playwright's original words rather than translating them into other media, and, although the author can give directions for all of these other elements, the dialogue is the only element that, according to tradition, must be given. Emphasis on the verbal exists even in the case of scripts that are remembered rather than deduced. George Bernard Shaw, for example, has lengthy and detailed stage directions, yet changing them does not seem to evoke the same response as changing or omitting passages of dialogue. Some directors, operating under this same double standard, immediately cross out all stage directions in a script but make the dialogue sacrosanct. According to this line of reasoning, a play is literary to the extent that it contains dialogue. The borrowing of script materials from various sources to make a verbal collage, the use of several playwrights, or the improvised creation of dialogue may alter the usual consistent literary style, but it does not eliminate the mental recreation of a script or the consideration of words at a level different from the other performance material.

There is some validity in this approach because priority given to dialogue, unless it is unusual, will emphasize what I have defined as the literary aspects of a production. Such a view of literary theatre lacks usefulness, however, because it is not comprehensive. As we have seen, it is possible to "read" a performance that has no dialogue; nonverbal theatre can also be literary. If "literary" is equated with the use of dialogue, all productions of the same script—whether a staged reading or an elaborately staged presentation—would be equally literary. Yet one production of a particular script may be more (or less) literary than another production of the same script.

How can this happen? As far as signs and symbols are concerned, it is important to decide whether quantity is of significance. In other words, is a production with many signs more literary than one with fewer signs? This is not so much a question of absolute numbers as it is of relative sign density. If many performance signs are added to those verbal signs of the script, the work of "reading" the presentation, and its literary quality, will be increased. This is true even if no new information is given by the added signs and they merely support in a redundant fashion the information presented in words. Increased sign redundancy will also make a performance more literary.

Obviously, one production may control the reading pattern more closely than another, even though both are directed according to reading patterns and both are, therefore, literary. One production might insert spectacular interludes or other material that cannot be read in a patterned manner. By adding theatrical material, certain scenes might be presented simultaneously in one production, making it less literary than one that followed a single, clear reading pattern.

As we have seen, the evocative power of a theatrical sign depends on the way it is presented as well as on what it represents. Just as the word "horse" may be said in a way that will stimulate mental imagery, various physical images of a horse may induce imagery to varying degrees (whereas a real horse will be the image rather than causing an image to occur in the imagination). Thus, one production of a particular script may work toward an extreme stimulation of imaginative images while another production of the same script does little or nothing with the image process.

In like manner, critical reference may be added to a script in production. A script that makes no value judgments about anything, that asks no critical consideration of any subject, may have a political, social, or moral slant given to it. This approach will make it more literary than it was intended to be. Thus it is not the script that decides the literary quality of a performance, and one production of a script may be much more literary than another production of the same script.

style as perceptual state

Except for such states as dream and hallucination, every experience "bonds together" the objective and the subjective. Part of the experience depends on the objective reality; part depends on and is created by the individual spectator. The thing that is "out there" and our response to it become fused. Ultimately, it is this fusion—the experience of the spectator—that concerns us. We need to "pry apart" the two aspects of the experience to analyze it. The concept of eye-movement analysis has already given us a tool.

Although, as the name indicates, the particular form of eye movement that we call "reading pattern" may be employed in receiving a message, it is not a part of that message. The path our eyes travel and the rate at which they move as they read a letter or a play do not alter the information communicated. Indeed, the reading pattern of all printed matter—books, magazines, newspapers, and so on—in the same language is more or less the same. Reading pattern is purely formal. It is one type of eye movement a spectator may employ.

As a particular type of eye movement extends through time, the perceiving organism is led to respond in a certain way. The physiological operation—in and of itself—creates a certain feeling tone that becomes a part of the experience. Unfocused or "syncretistic" vision produces one feeling tone; rapid, repeated, patterned movements another; random scanning yet another; and so on. We will call this process "induction." The performance induces the spectator to behave and, therefore, to feel in a certain way.

Once the pattern of induction has been established, eye-movement patterning may be seen as a model representing the way in which style, at least in its broadest terms, is experienced. In this model, style is not a configuration of characteristics belonging to the objective performance. When seen as the result of induction, style is perceptual state. Let us examine the question of style.

We may say, together with the *American Heritage Dictionary of the English Language*, that style is "the way in which something is said or done, as distinguished from its substance." Thus, in considering style, we are concerned with form rather than with content, the physical nature of the piece rather than the ideas expressed. There are two kinds of style: the specific style embodied in each particular work and general style, which involves several or more works, each of which manifests that general style. In neither case are we concerned with isolated details or moments. Style is a generalization. We recognize it when certain elements or relationships are repeated. Style is identified by multiple identities and/or similarities in the materials used and the way they are combined.

The complexity of performance as an artistic medium makes its stylistic analysis somewhat more difficult than those of the other arts. At the same time, a simple way to examine style in theatre is to compare it with other art forms. Just as we may consider visual style in painting, we may consider merely the visual style of a theatrical presentation. The historical relationship of much scenography and costume design to established and identifiable styles of painting does not need to be discussed here, nor does the reliance by directors on various styles of picturization and pictorial composition derived from painting, but it is enough, for now, to accept the possibility that a performance may be studied as a series of pictures. The style of each picture can be analyzed and categorized just as we analyze and categorize painting style. Pictorial style can be seen as one aspect of theatrical style.

In identifying pictorial style, we search for and categorize similarities and repetitions in the way materials and elements are combined and arranged. Selection of colors of a certain type, or quality, the repeated use of particular color harmonies, of a particular line, form, shape, brushstroke, and so on, all become aspects of style. An individual painting has its own style to the extent that it repeats elements not repeated in quite the same way in other works. It belongs to a general style—Impressionism, let us say—when it shares repeated details, such as the type of brushstroke, with other paintings; the repeated similarities occur in all the works in that general style and do not occur—at least not in the same configuration with other stylistic elements—in works outside that style. The point is that style is recognized not in the isolated occurrence of elements such as a specific line or a particular shape but in the repeated occurrence of these elements. Thus, even in a painting—which, as we have seen, is "read" by the eye—style may be considered to exist in time. It becomes manifest only through time, the time necessary for repeated similarities and identities to be recognized. In theatre as in the visual arts, eye-movement pattern is one of the elements of pictorial style. The particular way in which the eye moves over (or does not move over) the presented material becomes one dimension of the style of a performance. Different styles of theatre are distinguished, in part, by different eye-movement patterns that contribute to the overall pictorial style.

Of course, there is much more to a performance than just its pictorial style. We might speak of time style (the manner in which tempo, pace, pausing, and so forth are used), movement style, and auditory or sound style. In each case, the style is recognized by identities and similarities that reveal themselves through time. All of these, taken together, make up the style of the performance. The performance is grouped with other performances as having the same style if it shares with them the same repeated details.

We may even speak of ideational style. Ideational style does not refer to the specific sign-functions or ideas themselves but to repeated identities and similarities in the types or qualities of ideational material, in the way the material is encoded, and in the way syntax is used and developed. Since style is a generalization, different ideas may be expressed in the same ideational style; we need not understand the ideas to perceive the style.

It is clear that something similar to ideational style exists in everyday life: there are different manners or modes of thought. We do not think in the same way when we are drowsy, for example, as we do when we are wide awake. Drugs—including the alcohol, tobacco, and caffeine of common everyday life—alter the way we think. Although not all drugs work, of course, with the same force and control, the mental state created by each tends to remain the same for each person. It is repeatable, predictable, and identifiable. The single-point contemplative techniques of Zen and the whirling contemplative techniques of the Dervishes create particular and unusual states of mind. Different intellectual materials also induce different thoughts. The way the mind works—and feels—in mathematical problem-solving is different from the way it works when reading a poem; doing a crossword puzzle or a translation is different from reading a report. Not only does the mind work in different ways, but each mode of thought has its own affective tone or quality.

Now we come to the point at which eye-movement pattern may be seen as a model that enables us to understand style not as objective characteristics but as a state of mind. We join the concept of style as repeated identities and similarities existing in time to the concept of induction and the recognition of different modes of thought. If particular eye-movement patterns may—completely apart from the referential or nonreferential nature of the material being viewed—be considered physiologically to induce certain feeling tones that become part of the total experience, why cannot particular thinking patterns existing in theatre be seen—completely apart from the ideational content of the material involved—to create certain modes of thought, each with its own affective quality? Not only eye-movement pattern and ideational style but every element of style may be seen to be inductive, leading the spectator into a certain physiological process or operation.

Since each aspect of style is a generality functioning through time, each can be seen to induce a particular process in the observer. The spectator, that is, does not merely perceive the material but functions in accordance with the style of the material. Each mode of functioning has its own affective tone or quality. Since the overall style of the performance is a combination of several different stylistic dimensions—including eye-movement pattern and ideational style—the total functioning of the spectator is induced at many levels. The result is what I call a "perceptual state." Each style induces a particular perceptual state.

"Perceptual state" refers to the functioning of the entire organism, both body and mind. Indeed, fundamental to the concept is the symbiotic relationship between mind and body. As we have seen in considering different modes of thought, a particular physiological condition or process can induce a certain state of mind. For example, the total physical relaxation and the reduction of visual and auditory phenomena in single-point contemplation induce in the mind the dreamlike alpha state, whose brain-wave patterns are recognizable and identifiable. Conversely, the mind affects the body. Remembering a painful experience can cause muscular tension, imaginatively involving the mind in an athletic activity is used by some as an anesthetic, and so on. Neither the mind nor the body alone creates a perceptual state. An unconscious person would not perceive; it is impossible to prevent the physiological from making its contribution—although the condition has been approached in sensory deprivation work. Any perceptual state is produced and sustained by both the mind and the body.

A symbiotic or reciprocal relationship also exists between the theatrical performance and the perceptual state. The style of the performance induces, after a period of time, a particular perceptual state. That perceptual state organizes thoughts and feelings in a particular way. It acts as a container and frame of reference that focuses, organizes, and processes details in its own way and has its own perceived quality and character. The performance demands to be perceived in a particular way; the perceiving organism agrees and continues to process all incoming material in that particular way. This experience is open to some extent to introspection. We refer to it when we speak of "getting with," "getting into," any work of art. We become "involved in" or "absorbed by" the work. When we end this involvement, we sometimes notice—even with a degree of surprise and shock—the adjustment necessary to perceive in their usual way the materials of everyday life. Sometimes the induced perceptual state persists, and we continue to experience and "process" everyday life in the same way we had been experiencing the work of art.

Let us look at examples of perceptual states that have been induced in theatre. The opening of Richard Wagner's Festspielhaus in Beyreuth in 1876 was one of the single most important moments in the history of theatre—not because, as some say, it introduced the fan-shaped auditorium that has been so prevalent in the last century but because Wagner had created a "dream machine." This was the first theatre designed not for practical (usually economic) concerns but to induce in the spectator a particular perceptual state—a state modeled on the dream. The auditorium was darkened—something we tend to take for granted but which was an innovation at the time. The sound of the invisible orchestra rose from a specially designed pit, the "mystic gulf" that made ambiguous the distance between the audience and the performance. A series of prosceniums that decreased in size framed the front of the auditorium and the stage and created an optical illusion, distorting perspective and making the performers seem larger than they really were. The dreamlike perceptual state calculatedly induced in the spectator by these architectural effects was independent of the particular content of the operas presented. Its effect would be basically the same for every production done at the Beyreuth Festspielhaus.

The Symbolists continued this interest in the dream. Their productions were long and slow, the actors moved little and spoke in monotones, scrims and subdued lighting made the stage vague and indistinct. All these elements combined to put the spectator into the contemplative state in which muscles are relaxed, breathing and pulse rate are reduced, the mind "floats" without applying and using logic, perhaps images rise spontaneously—as in a dream.

Naturalism, too, contributed to a subdued, hushed attitude in the spectator. At the Moscow Art Theatre, Stanislavski banned latecomers and eliminated the curtain calls between acts. An eavesdropping audience, viewing the performance through an imaginary fourth wall, should be polite and self-effacing. It should not intrude. The style of the production should not be broken. This semireligious atmosphere of the art theatres was found, too, in museums, where people felt they had to whisper—as if in church—even though the work presented was inanimate and could not be disturbed.

Edward Bullough (in "Psychical Distance," 1913) was perhaps the first to analyze this "art trance," as Laurie Anderson has recently called it. Bullough recognized that a person could intentionally put him or herself into a detached, contemplative state of consciousness. When viewing a fog at sea from a ship, for example, one could attend only to the sensory aspects of the experience—the quality of the fog, the muffled hooting of the fog horns, the impact and sound of the waves, and so on. This meant ignoring or detaching oneself from the practical aspects of the experience—fog at sea could be dangerous in Bullough's day. By attending to the formal and ignoring or rejecting the practical, a person might reach an aesthetic state whether or not art was actually involved.

Thus Bullough could establish a continuum that stretched from practical involvement to a completely detached, uninvolved, and disinterested state. Figuratively, he began this scale of "aesthetic distance" at the object, so that practical involvement became "under distance" and detachment became "over distance." The ideal aesthetic distance was at the middle of the continuum—neither overdistanced nor underdistanced.

Bullough also realized that if spectators could, to some extent, control and manipulate their attitude, the characteristics of the thing perceived also affected aesthetic distance. It was more difficult, for example, to achieve the proper aesthetic distance when sexual or political material was involved. Bullough was speaking, however, about only one perceptual state, and he was taking for granted that it applied to all art. Art does not need to be viewed "aesthetically," though, and not all art seeks an aesthetic "distance."

Futurists reacted against the hypnotic dream theatre. They broke down the fourth wall of Naturalism, the "barrier" between stage and auditorium, provoking and insulting the spectators. The perceptual state induced included self-awareness and self-concern. It was alert and critical.

Expressionism investigated yet another perceptual state. The screams and contorted bodies of the actors, the strident colors and harsh contrasts of light, the abrupt changes of tone all contributed in creating a focused nervous tension in the spectator. Physical empathy, which will be discussed a little later, was an important element in the experience.

The induction of these perceptual states should not be confused with the representation of a state of mind. Much early art that appears nonrepresentational was actually an attempt to represent something that could not be perceived in the external world: a state of mind. This, too, would fit our communication model. Induction, on the other hand, relates to the functioning of the spectator and is unrelated to any message that might be conveyed. A performance may be "about" a dream without inducing a dreamlike state; the state may be induced with no reference to a dream. If Richard Foreman's productions are about his or a state of mind, they also induce a distinct perceptual state because of their unique style.

Here we begin to see the outlines of a typography of perceptual states. Because several of the extreme positions have been investigated and established, we can discern the parameters, the continua, by which various states may be described and measured. Alertness of mind and body, muscular tension/relaxation, heart and pulse rate, the degree to which hearing and vision are focused, the amount of self-awareness, the logicality of thought, and so on all become dimensions of the perceptual state. This analytical approach would not distinguish between literary and nonliterary theatre; both produce perceptual states in the spectator. It does distinguish clearly, however, between theatre as literature and theatre as performance.

Several years ago, I attempted to experiment with the concept of style as a perceptual state. One hypothesis was that the performer, being in a particular perceptual state different from that of the spectator, induces, after a certain period of time, the spectator to change his or her perceptual state to that of the performer. To test this hypothesis, I had to be able to measure the perceptual state of both the performer and the spectator. Biofeedback machines that indicate the state of brain-wave functions were one way to approach this measure. I borrowed a biofeedback machine. If I could learn to put myself into a particular state—the machine was designed to teach someone how to enter the alpha state—and could perform in that state while monitoring the brain waves of the spectators, I might be able to validate the hypothesis. Unfortunately, the equipment was not subtle enough. Any muscular movement, even the movement of the closed eye, caused static and prevented accurate measurement. One could not watch a performance, much less perform, while using the equipment. Testing the hypothesis awaits more sophisticated equipment.

Questioning what seemed to be an unwritten law limiting a play to a single style, I created *A Style Play* that moved from one style to another and staged it in my apartment. There were four actors in the cast; a full house—we did about twenty performances—was twelve invited spectators. When the play began, the room in which the audience sat was empty. The only light came through the windows. Two men appeared and whispered to each other. Apparently, they were waiting for the person who lived in the apartment. Looking out the window, they saw her coming and disappeared. After a moment—the apartment was on the twelfth floor—the door to the hall was unlocked from the outside, and the woman entered. The scene was as realistic as it could be made. The next scene was done in the style of Japanese No theatre with two musicians, costumes, chanted dialogue, and sylized movement. Then the continuing story was told through puppets, in verse melodrama, as a farce, and so on. After numerous changes of style, A Style Play ended with the four actors reading aloud reviews of the production ostensibly from different papers and journals. Written, of course, in different styles, two of the reviews were very positive and laudatory; two were negative and damning.

In doing the play, two very practical aspects of style became apparent. In the first place, time is not the only element necessary to "get into" a style. Each of the sections lasted long enough—the entire play ran about an hour and a half—for the spectator to respond to it, for the style to induce a particular state. Once the first change in style took place, however, the tendency was to "hang back," to anticipate the changes and watch for them from a distance. Just as some may smoke marijuana without getting high, a particular style does not guarantee a specific perceptual state. It merely makes it possible. All of the style changes in A Style Play created only one perceptual state rather than many. Style became an intellectual element rather than an affective one.

The second thing that became apparent from A Style Play was the difficulty for performers in switching from one style to another. Changes may, of course, be made easily and quickly at a technical level, but—as the experiment with the biofeedback equipment indicates—I was also concerned with a "deep style" that involved the performers' entire functional state at an ideational/physiological level. Functional state for a performer corresponds, then, to the concept of perceptual state in the spectator. In these terms, if an actor is "in" a particular functional state, everything he or she does will be a manifestation of that state, and the style will be consistent. If actors do not change the basic state, they will not be able to change the style, even when they use completely different techniques. A corollary of this formulation posits that the technique related to a particular style induces the performer to reach a specific functional state, but, here again, time is necessary.

Performers who did not appear in one scene of A Style Play could make a much more complete transition than they could if they appeared—as they almost always did—in two consecutive scenes. The nature of the production forced the actors, as well as the spectators, into an intellectual detachment and into one functional mode.

To work, among other things, on changing the actor's state of functioning, I decided to try hypnotism. The hypothesis was that an actor in a somnambulistic state could, when directed, switch functional states much more quickly, easily, and completely than could a nonhypnotized actor. Many of the rational obstacles and the tendency toward intellectual detachment would be eliminated. Several early sessions of the Structuralist Workshop, a theatre group I formed, were devoted to hypnotism. We were trying to find two or three examples of that supposed one in ten who could go into a deep trance, but a woman who had had several years of experience with hypnotism was unable to induce a somnambulistic state in any of the volunteers. As a subject, I was able to reach only a low-level state of suggestibility, which was induced by a record. I studied hypnotism and tried to become a hypnotist. I, too, was unsuccessful. Although I still think the concept has validity and that somnambulism could be used in many ways in creating performance, I abandoned active pursuit of the idea when I met a psychologist who for many years had used hypnotism in working at a Veterans' Administration hospital. He said that he had never been able to put anyone into a somnambulistic state.

Finally, let us consider a group of more or less well-known phenomena that also involve a bond between spectator and performer. As in the concept of perceptual state, a procedure or process is established in the observer. We can call them psychophysical mechanisms.

Projection, a concept derived from psychiatry, is, according to Webster, "the unconscious act or process of ascribing to others one's own ideas, impulses or emotions." This may be contrasted with the process of identification, in which the spectator unconsciously accepts as his or her own the ideas, impulses, emotions, characteristics, and behavior of a character. In one case, spectators project their personality onto the performance; in the other, they take on a personality suggested by the performance. Analytically, these concepts could be useful if we were able to construct continua to measure their strength or the degree to which they were functioning and the material that related to that functioning.

Both identification and projection would seem to be facilitated by material in congruence with the spectator's own life. It is easier to project one's own feelings into a character or situation that one knows well and understands; it is difficult to identify with unfamiliar characters and ones unlike oneself. By these standards, we could agree with the proposition that it is easier, in general, to identify with and/or project into the character of Willy Loman than it is to relate in these same ways to Hamlet.

The continua constructed according to these principles would be somewhat different for individual spectators, reflecting the specifics of their lives and personalities. A woman, according to this principle, would more easily identify with and/or project into a female character; a man would relate more easily with a man. Individual differences and personal psychodynamics become very important, however. A man who, at least unconsciously, wanted to be a woman could project/identify more easily with a female character and vice versa. People who did not like their own lives and/or personalities might project/identify more easily with unfamiliar material, and so on.

This does not mean we should abandon the concept of continua for identification and projection. All of our continua relating to the experience of a performance have been generalizations constructed for everyone or for the "average" person. Such continua, however, could be constructed for each individual; they would, of course, be different from the general scale.

Whereas identification relates only to characters, projection also applies to situations. We may imaginatively put ourselves into a particular place. We do not "identify with" a landscape, for example, or an incident. In a film we are watching, a swimmer is enjoying himself. It is a beautiful night; the water of the ocean is exhilarating. We know from the story, however, that other swimmers have been attacked by sharks. We know, because we have been shown glimpses of it, that there is a shark nearby. The swimmer swims happily. Discordant music on the sound-track—unheard by the swimmer—becomes louder. We may project ourselves into the situation and into the swimming figure. We do not, however, identify with the swimmer. We do not take on his ideas, impulses, emotions, and so on. The swimmer is happy. He knows nothing of the shark. We project ourselves into the situation as we understand it, not as the swimmer understands it. In that situation, we "use" our own feelings, rather than those of the character. Thus we can distinguish between situations that use identification and those that do not.

Although we may project ourselves quickly into a situation, identification, because it is with a character, is generally a longer process, becoming "deeper," stronger, and more complex as we learn more and more about the character. It is easier, then, to identify with a leading character who is on stage for a long time. (Time is particularly necessary if the character is unlike ourselves.) Thus by the time Hamlet dies, we may have identified with him much more completely than, say, with Horatio. (At any rate, we probably would have to make a choice. It seems that identification—as opposed to projection—usually occurs with only one character.) Of course, identification is as much with the personality of the performer as with the assumed character. When we leave a movie theatre feeling as if we were Clint Eastwood, say, or Goldie Hawn, it is the actor's idiosyncratic behavior that has left its traces on us as much as the character developed in the particular film.

There is a problem here. Is it not empathy that we have been discussing? Webster says it is. According to him, empathy is "the projection of one's own personality into the personality of another . . . , the ability to share in another's emotions or feelings," and also "the projection of one's own personality into an object." The word is commonly used in this way. This is not the scientific or aesthetic use of the word, however, and if we make empathy synonymous with projection and identification, we will have no distinct term for that special kind of empathy, which is significantly different.

In 1897, Violet Paget—using the pen name Vernon Lee, because, one assumes, it was easier to be published and to be taken seriously if one was believed to be a man—made, in an article titled "Beauty and Ugliness," what was apparently the first conceptualization of empathy theory in English. She described how we say that a mountain rises or a line extends although there is no objective movement in the mountain or the line. The movement, Paget/Lee said, is within us. She was calling attention to the way a physical response in the observer—the movement of the head up and back to look at the mountain, the movement of the eyes as they followed the line—was projected into the objective world and seen as a quality or characteristic of it. This is quite different from "the projection of one's own personality." At least, the distinction is useful in the analysis of theatre.

Paget's work was apparently independent of that of Theodor Lipps, who had already published on empathy theory in German. Instead of speaking of objects and the natural world, Lipps described a performance situation in "Empathy, Inner Imitation, and Sense Feeling." (It may be found, together with the "Vernon Lee" and Bullough's previously mentioned "Psychical Distance" in *A Modern Book of Esthetics* edited by Melvin Rader.) Lipps wrote,

[F]rom my seat in the theatre, I observe a dance which is performed upon the stage. In this case it is impossible for me to take part in the dance. Nor do I have the desire to dance; I am not in the mood for it. Both my situation and attitude prevent any bodily movements. But this does not eliminate my inner activity.

The contemplation of the observed movement awakens a corresponding "self-activity," and we have "Einfühlung" or empathy.

Psychology, too, uses empathy to describe a physical response. It is
illustrated, for example, by the way spectators involuntarily twist their
own bodies while watching a pole vaulter attempt to clear the bar. This
can be distinguished from conscious physical projection, as when a
golfer twists in trying to influence the roll of the putted ball through
"sympathetic magic."

Empathy, then, is purely physical response and the projection of sensations of movement rather than the projection of personality. Here
again, we may construct a continuum that indicates the degree to which
empathy is involved in a performance. It is the easiest to do with dance.
Unless we respond empathetically to everything, we do not empathize
with, say, a person walking down the street. At least we can say there is
little empathetic response to ordinary everyday activity. When postmodern dance, then, uses ordinary movement that requires no technique or training, it is not perceived empathetically. When ballet dancers,
on the other hand, move in ways that are unusual, we may posit that
they are highly empathetic. Empathy is a useful tool for spectators in
"understanding" movement that is unfamiliar to them.

In the same way, we may say that energetic movement—as in wres-
tling or pole vaulting—is more empathetic than relaxed movement.
A dance involving leaps and pirouettes is more empathetic than a gentle,
uninflected dance. Thus the movements of the Expressionist actor and
the Neo-Expressionism of Grotowski-style actors are more empathetic
than acting using the Stanislavski system or the American method. So the
consideration of psychophysical mechanisms has led us back to style.
The continua measuring projection, identification, and empathy may be
seen, at least in part, as additional dimensions of style.

The concept of perceptual states suggests one possibility for new theatre. One may see theatre as a machine for creating and inducing new
perceptual states. Perceptual states are, of course, induced by nature and
the natural world. Nature, however, no matter how rich and diverse, is
limited. It has given us only a certain range of experience. The history of
theatre has given us other, nonnatural, artificial perceptual states that
add to the possibilities of our experience. Theatre based on the natural
model can increase these possibilities even more, creating perceptual
states that are completely new. Humans change because of new experiences. The change opens new possibilities for experience. It is an ever-
expanding progression.

the social context

Criticism is not part of theatre. It is part of the social context of theatre. It mediates between theatre, considered as experience, and the larger world in which the theatrical event exists. That is why a discussion of criticism belongs in this second section, which is devoted to certain aspects of the social context of performance.

The "question of efficacy" that is asked in the second chapter of this part concerns the practical impact of theatre on its spectators and the larger "indirect" audience. We are not concerned here with experience but with transtheatrical application in the "real" world. This, too, is a sociological investigation.

In the third part, the avant-garde is presented as a sociological phenomenon rather than as something determined and defined by aesthetic and stylistic standards.

Behind all three pieces in this section, which tends to be more emotional than the first, lies a deep and only partly conscious involvement. Although I write about theatre in general, my personal interest is only with theatre as an art, and the experience of art for me, I realize, is something close to what I take to be the religious experience. (This sounds old-fashioned, but there is a need to explain "where I'm coming from" in this part.) Art, like the religious experience, is private, personal, "hermetic"—sealed off from particular practical exigencies. It *feels* true and useful, but the truth cannot be proved by the intellect, and the usefulness cannot be applied in any tangible way. The "truth" of art, like that of religion, is "revealed." It is not available to the logical mind. Although this "truth" feels universal, one knows intellectually that it is not. Buddha was not more or less "correct" than St. John of the Cross. You are not more or less correct than I am, either religiously or artistically.

Individual artists may "believe" in one art—the art they do—

but that does not mean they are unable to appreciate and value other arts. Just as it is possible—even if it is not accomplished everywhere—to accept all the contradictions in our vast and complex religious heritage, we may accept simultaneously all the myriad contradictions in our vast and complex artistic heritage. Yet most, or at least many, people do not do this. The underlying emotions of this second section come from a belief that the social context of theatre in our time is in many ways repressive and intolerant of the private experience of art in performance.

Since we are thinking of society, repression, and intolerance, let us change the metaphor. Art (and religion) as personal and private—nonsocial—experience may be compared to sex. The avant-garde described in the third section of this part is a social minority, just as homosexuals and lesbians are minorities. Within each of those minorities lie others with even more specialized tastes. The repressiveness evidenced in our society by even the Supreme Court toward minority sexual experience becomes related in my mind to the social repression of artistic experience. I feel the urge to defend the right to certain experiences even when I do not myself "believe" in those experiences. William James's *The Varieties of Religious Experience* is one of my favorite books, although I am not a religious person. James was a scientist interested in the unusual because it explained a lot about life. Thus though the approach of this section of *A Formalist Theatre* is as programmatically logical as Part I, the result is more obviously emotional.

the critical screen

There is no such thing as good or bad acting. There is only acting that we or someone else thinks/feels is good or bad. Value does not inhere in the performance. Objectively, there are only technical and quantitative differences between different actors and different styles of acting. All kinds and degrees of acting are equally good, and no point on the acting/not-acting continuum elaborated in the first chapter is better or worse than any other. All value judgments are, by definition, subjective.

Therefore, criticism functions as a social screen to separate us from the actual theatrical production. Much of the time it discourages us from attending by ascribing negative values to the work. In this case the screen becomes a shield, keeping us from the experience. If we go to a performance after reading something about it, after reading something ascribing values to that type of theatre, or even after reading an evaluation of theatre in general, our own value responses are not pure. They are, to some extent, colored and changed by what we have read. This screen filters our experience for us. It leads us to think and feel in a way we would not do without the screen. We have no need for the critical screen.

On January 11, 1966, a review by Clive Barnes, entitled "Village Disaster," was published in the *New York Times:*

Total disaster struck the Judson Church in Washington Square last night. Correction: total nothingness struck the Judson Church in Washington Square last night, struck it with the squelchy ignominy of a tomato against a pointless target.

The occasion, such as it was, was announced as a "Dance Concert of Old and New Works by David Gordon, Yvonne Rainer and Steve Paxton." One hoped, piously and, as Scarpin says in *Tosca,* in church, too, that there was more old than new.

To take the best first: there was a slight sense in Yvonne Rainer's work. She had a modest, no, more than modest technique, and she looked as though there was a certain talent infusing her movements. Her collaborators, the sad Mr. Paxton and the wry-faced Mr. Gordon, also looked trained and ready.

Choreography seemed outside their ken, and the results were only amusing in the camp way of the ghastly, the terrible, the totally undistinguished. While this is sickly amusing when unintended, add intention and the results are merely pitiable.

Among the dancers was Robert Rauschenberg, the erstwhile painter and collaborator with Merce Cunningham. On his own he looked a lay figure, like a plump, willing curate at a Sunday school outing, trying to enter the fun but failing.

The most interesting event of the evening was when someone, through the long extent of a blissfully boring dance number, threw from the top of the church a succession of wooden laths. Plomp, plomp went the laths and for a time, as these in rigid succession floated earthwards, one had a visual sense of something happening.

For the rest, the evening was nothing but the exercise of puerile egocentric minds in the futile quest of shocking the already unshockable. Poor little darlings! And poor dance, that our self-styled avant-garde should be reduced to this pitiful, adolescent caterwauling. But already we raise our voice too loud.

With their feeble little pomposities and vainglorious hopes, their silly, tiny tape machines, and half-assimilated techniques, these eager children of the dance explosion are presumably playing their predestined parts. Yet one wishes they would play them less obviously.

This is not a typical review. It is much too forceful, too emotional, and too completely negative to be typical. Yet it can be used to exemplify how criticism functions.

After the Judson Church performance in 1966, David Gordon gave up dancing and choreography until 1971. Even if he had not returned to the art, he would have made an extremely important contribution to the history of dance—in the concert that was reviewed by Barnes and in earlier work. David Gordon, Yvonne Rainer, and Steve Paxton were three of the key figures in the development of postmodern dance, which is among the most important artistic innovations of our time. Even without historical dimension, however, the review can be used to represent the destructive possibilities of evaluation.

Barnes was not wrong or incorrect in the review. He was describing not the performances themselves but how he felt about the performances. There is no reason to think that he was inaccurate. Evaluation is neither right nor wrong. All evaluation is right, correct, for the person who does it. If one person thinks a performance is "good" and another thinks it is "bad," both are right. All evaluations of a performance are equally correct.

This distinguishes personal, subjective, evaluative response from description, analysis, and ascription of significance. Obviously, Barnes did not think the occasion or type of work significant. Just as clearly, he was incorrect. The aesthetics of postmodern dance have interested many people and have been discussed widely. It has had wide influence. Its originators have become well known. Postmodern dance has established its historical importance. Its success is completely apart from whether any one person liked or disliked it. One may dislike the work of Picasso; no one may rightly say that he was unimportant or insignificant.

Just as clearly, the review illustrates how the avant-garde is almost always measured by traditional standards. Barnes knew that the work was attempting to be innovative, yet he used technique and talent as evaluative criteria. A "modest technique" and "a certain talent" are ascribed to Yvonne Rainer. Neither technique nor talent exists, however, until a form has been developed and codified. There are certain *kinds* of technique; there is talent *for* certain defined activities. Once methods and procedures have been developed and codified, we may say that a technique exists. It can be taught and learned. Once a particular activity has been defined and its techniques formulated, we may be able to identify a talent for that activity. Those who can do the activity easily, with the least effort and study, have the most talent for it. But neither technique nor talent is a standard that can be applied to the developing avant-garde. There, nothing is yet defined and codified, and anything is possible. One indication of traditionally oriented criticism is the positive emphasis it puts on technique and talent. It clings to the known and established, to the standards it has learned, and uses the characteristics of the old work to reject the new and the innovative, to which talent and technique do not apply.

Theatrical criticism, as we know it, is primitive and naive, arrogant, and immoral. We accept that this should be so because it always has been so. Mental and cultural inertia justifies nothing, however. Criticism should be changed.

There are two aspects to criticism: the passing of value judgments and analysis. It is the former that will be questioned here. Indeed, the word "criticism" will be used to refer specifically to the act of publishing statements of value. (One definition given by Webster is "a finding fault; censuring; disapproval.") In speaking of critics, we are not referring only to reviewers but to anyone who publicly evaluates and passes value judgments upon any aspect of theatre. Thus, the evaluative and analytical functions will be considered as separate and distinct; "analysis" will be opposed to "criticism" rather than included in it. In these terms, it is not merely a change that will be asked of criticism. Criticism as value judgment is a harmful anachronism and should be eliminated completely.

(Before attempting to explain and argue these statements, it should be pointed out that many teachers are actually classroom critics. When we are discussing criticism, we are also discussing teaching. Much teaching of theatre is also primitive and naive, arrogant, and immoral.)

These are serious charges. It is not necessary to accept all of them; each of the claims—and there will be another—is significant and should be sufficient in itself. Nor are these claims value judgments or mere aspersions. Each has a logical base that will be explained.

Let us consider the claims one by one. "Primitive and naive" refers to the fact that most criticism is based on a simple, unsophisticated, but false assumption about the world: that everyone can, should, or does perceive the same phenomenal existence. "Even though you may have a different opinion about it or a different value of it," the position holds, "what we perceive is the same for both of us." The consideration of value rests on this base. If the experience of a thing is understood to vary from person to person, the valuation of that thing is expected to vary, but criticism is based to a great extent on the false assumption that what is seen and heard by one person is what is seen and heard by another when presented with the same sensory input. This, however, is not the case.

There are countless examples. Let us use the Seashore tests or "measures of musical talent" developed by Carl Seashore. On one of these tests, subjects are given two musical notes; they are asked to indicate whether the second note has the same pitch as the first or whether it is different. On another of the tests, two short rhythms are compared, and so on. Some people do very well on these tests. Some few even have a perfect score. But most people, of course, are not able to make fine distinctions, and the results plot out on the usual bell-shaped normal distribution curve: median scores are the most common, and the numbers of people achieving a particular score decrease as the scores move away in both directions from the median.

If asked, we could say whether we liked or disliked one of the notes or whether we preferred one rhythm to another. When presented with even a single sound or a single color, we automatically evaluate it. Every perception has a value attribute. It carries with it, as an inherent part of the experience, a particular value component. It has a degree of "good-bad," "attraction-repulsion," "beautiful-ugly," and so on along with its qualities. Thus values are fused with the perceptual world.

Therefore it is important to stress the simple and obvious point that, as demonstrated by the Seashore tests, people do not hear and see the same things when presented with the same sensory material; because of this, they cannot be expected to have the same value responses. A person, for example, has a particular value response to a particular note. If presented with two different notes, he or she cannot discriminate between them, then both have the same value for that person. To a person who can make the discrimination, the notes have different values. A human being is a complex organism, and if equipment were available to measure one's total value response it would show that each person's pattern was, like fingerprints, unique.

Psychological tests have been developed to investigate many different aspects of perceptual and cognitive ability ranging from thresholds and scanning patterns to memory and so-called "IQ." The normal distribution curve of the Seashore tests is typical. On each scale, a few people are found to have unusual perceptual and cognitive abilities. They literally do not perceive and understand the same "things," although there is a high degree of similarity among average responses.

A common experiment in a basic psychology course is to compare accounts of an unannounced but planned incident: the banishment of a student for cheating, the "shooting" of the professor, and so forth. Of course, the reports of these prototheatrical events vary widely. As every lawyer knows, eyewitnesses do not see the same accident, the same crime. Why should criticism be based on the assumption that everyone sees the same performance?

The point is not to demand that all critics be tested for perceptual acuity and/or verifiable mental functions such as short-term memory. Indeed, the dimensions of the theatrical experience are so numerous and complex, it would seem statistically impossible that anyone could be in, say, the top percentile on all of them. (If tests were given to all critics, would only that one critic who scored the highest—that "most sensitive" one—be allowed to pass judgment? Since most people would have median scores, should not the critic, too, have average perception?)

A favorite parable of critics is the story of the emperor's new clothes. Thinking he is wearing remarkable new clothing, the emperor rides through the city. Because of social pressure, no one will admit to not seeing the clothes. Finally, a young and innocent child blurts out, "The emperor is naked!" Of course, the critic identifies with the child, believing that everyone sees the truth, as the critic does, but will not admit it for social reasons. This is particularly true for the avant-garde. When something is incomprehensible to critics, they cannot understand how anyone else can "get anything" out of the work. The others must be pretending.

It is natural, even innocent, to assume that everyone perceives the world as we do. This is why most criticism can be called "primitive and naive." It is not an intelligent or sophisticated position.

There are two ways in which words indicating value can be used. One is the personal, and the other is the pseudo-objective. In its primitive state, criticism often does not distinguish between them or make clear which use is being employed. The personal form refers to the critic's own taste, emotional reaction, and so on. The pseudo-objective form attempts to refer to the known taste of others and can be intellectual rather than emotional.

The fact that values are ultimately subjective does not mean that there is complete disagreement about them. On the broad, general, and unrefined level at which values can be writen about and discussed, there is often agreement. Thus a general consensus on the type of stimuli referred to by some words that convey value gives these words a pseudo-objectivity. Most people in a society will designate a particular woman as "beautiful," for example; there are many other women that few in that society would describe as "beautiful."

Not all value-indicators have a consensual character. Female beauty is a good example because it is one of the most easily recognized. A "beautiful" dress, for example, or a "beautiful" lamp would not be so objectively descriptive. Their characteristics are not as narrowly limited or defined by the culture. The qualities they could *not* refer to are less numerous. Again, we could construct a continuum, this one stretching from the completely subjective to the completely objective. Degrees of pseudo-objectivity would occupy the middle of the scale.

The use of such value-indicators can be studied sociologically, scientifically, and, therefore, objectively. Value systems can be established empirically if one is willing to use the norms of a particular population as authority. An opinion poll could be taken, for example, that would demonstrate (prove) that Marilyn Monroe—still "living" in her films and photographs—is considered to be "beautiful" in our society. This would give her beauty a limited, cultural, or "pseudo"-objectivity. "Objective" means "independent of human emotions and opinions," and even when a value system is scientifically verified, it is still based on personal emotions and opinions. It is culturally relative and will change as emotions and opinions change. The "beautiful" woman that Rubens painted and the "beautiful" woman photographed in the last century are quite different from the "beautiful" woman of today.

Of course, we may think in terms of norms even if they are not scientifically verified. It may be our opinion that many or most people would consider that Marilyn Monroe is "beautiful," and we can use the term in that pseudo-objective sense. If I claim that Marilyn Monroe is "beautiful" because she appeals to my own personal taste, I am basing the statement on my emotions, but if I claim that she is objectively or normatively beautiful—that this characteristic has no dependence upon my own emotions or lack of them—it is a matter of opinion. Judgment has shifted from emotion to opinion, but until it is free of both emotion and opinion it cannot be termed "objective."

It is possible, then, to determine intellectually that a woman is "beautiful" without being attracted to her or finding her visually interesting. It is possible to dislike a "beautiful" painting or a "beautiful" performance. The same value-ascribing word may be used emotionally (to refer to a personal response) or intellectually (to refer to assumed or deduced standards). Yet critics seldom indicate the way in which they are ascribing value. This, of course, causes problems in communication.

In most cases, critics assume that the problem does not exist. They assume that their subjective response matches and fits within the objectified value standards of their society—that what they *feel* as beautiful is what is *thought* to be beautiful by the members of the society. In general terms, this is possible. One may assume that "normal" and "average" people of a particular society will tend to have the same general value response to the same thing or event. But it is only true in general. Thinking about values in a normative way overlooks or ignores all of the nonnormative examples. This is naive and primitive. After all, a norm is a statistical concept; few or even none may be represented by it in actuality.

(It may be said that the confusion of personal and pseudo-objective statements of value can be explained by convention. In conversation, we often say "It was good" when we mean "I liked it." Our friends understand us. The pseudo-objective phrase is conventionally understood to represent the personal one. Although this may be perfectly clear and acceptable in conversation, where familiarity with the speaker and the availability of many nonverbal indicators of meaning may make the convention obvious, it is not as easily accepted in written criticism. Enough criticism has been clear about the distinction to eliminate automatic acceptance of the convention. There is no reason why a person should write "It was good" when meaning "I liked it.")

Criticism is also primitive and naive if it assumes that value exists in the thing perceived—that value is objective. George Santayana was speaking against this common view before 1900. In *The Sense of Beauty*, he explains that "beauty is a value, that is, it is not a perception of a matter of fact or of a relation: it is an emotion." In other words, value, as an emotion, resides in the perceptor and not in the thing perceived. Since it is an inherent part of the experience of the objective world, it is objectified and projected into that world. Santayana defined "beauty" as "pleasure regarded as the quality of the thing." Accordingly, one could say that ugliness is pain regarded as the quality of the thing and that all values are emotions regarded as qualities of the thing. Theodore Lipps phrased it slightly differently: "The esthetic enjoyment," he wrote, "is not enjoyment of an object, but enjoyment of a self."

This is the universal nature of experience. Perception and value are inseparably fused. Value is experienced as residing in the thing perceived, rather than as something added by the perceiving organism. This is true even when a person does not believe that this is the way the world works. Just as a person who does not believe in free will experiences free will, the person who does not believe that things have an inherent value still perceives value to inhere in things. It is a primitive and naive attitude.

If nothing is inherently beautiful or ugly, good or bad, and value exists in the one who perceives rather than in the thing perceived, theatre critics are either naive or dishonest when they ascribe values to a performance. In either case, it is an arrogant act. Naive critics believe that the values they perceive are "real" and should be perceived by everyone; those who do not react as they do are not as "sensitive," as "perceptive," as "insightful," and so forth. This is the cliché of the critic as a god or superman who sees the "truth" where others do not. The critic who realizes that value is projected into the phenomenal world and who still continues to write as if values were objective is also arrogant. Knowing that the reactions of others are equally valid, they give their own a status that they know they cannot have.

Arrogance verges on narcissism in those critics who are merely giving "their own response" to a performance. If, as Lipps says, artistic enjoyment is "the enjoyment of a self," these people have a need to make that self public. They value it highly. It, not the work of art, is of primary importance. It becomes a screen, separating art and audience.

The third charge against criticism is that of immorality. There is an abstract standard by which negative criticism can be judged to be immoral. Saying "no" to any work of art can be seen as destructive when the view is projected socially. Of course, individual negative reactions are quite common. Most people will find most art to be dissatisfying to some degree. But what is negative to one is positive to another. Why should the possibility of a positive experience be denied? Why should there be the attempt to keep others from that experience or to persuade them that they have been "wrong"?

Of course, as a moral judgment this claim is based on a certain standard of ethics. If one senses an abstract power or energy in life, the liking of something may be seen as complimenting and aiding that positive flow; disliking something may be sensed as blocking or repressing the flow. Negative criticism works against the "life force." "Never say 'no' to anything" is an ethical and spiritual admonition.

(This position may seem paradoxical. The deprecation of criticism is, in itself, "saying 'no' to something." But the "life force"—as much of a moral absolute as any other standard—cannot be asked to turn upon itself. That would prohibit, among other things, saying "no" to murder. According to this moral position, negative criticism differs from murder only in degree.)

In these terms, positive criticism—anything that will help someone to like a work of art more or to "get something" from the experience—functions entirely differently than does negative criticism. There are other moral standards that weigh against both negative and positive criticism, however. These derive from the belief that no one should impose values or opinions upon anyone else. Every normal person—there may be grounds to exclude abnormalities such as the psychopathic personality—perceives value. Even the so-called feral child, who has grown up in the forest among wolves and knows neither language nor civilization, would like certain things and dislike others. Each person has a value system related to his or her own psychological identity and pattern of exchange with the world. Aesthetically, this system is neither right nor wrong, good nor bad. Aesthetically, all values exist only for the individual who feels, senses, or perceives those values. Aesthetically, one person's values are as correct as another's, and their integrity should be respected.

This could be called "democracy of taste." In a democracy, all are equal and freedom is respected. Critics are involved, intentionally or not, in a "fascism of taste." Under fascism, one person or party rules; standardization and conformity are imposed by dictate.

How and to what extent can values be imposed by one person or another? Values tend to be imposed most easily when the auditor of the statements cannot or does not check them against his or her own experience. In the absence of contradictory information, value judgments tend to be accepted. If you go to a play with a friend and discuss your reactions afterward, the impact of your friend's statements is much different than it would be if you had never seen the play. We tend to ascribe authority (or authoritativeness) to those with whom we agree, but in the absence of disagreement we tend to accept. How much theatre criticism is "validated" in this way? Relatively few people see most performances compared to the number who read about them; most of us read about many more performances than we actually attend. Once a performance has ended its run, it—unlike a film—is unavailable for criticial comparisons; only the critic's value judgments remain.

Certainly, the authority of almost-anonymous written criticism seems to be greater than are personal value judgments offered in conversation. The written word has its proverbial power. (Indeed, this may be what attracts some people to the practice of criticism.) The same statements made in conversation or even in a personal letter are qualified and their private meanings made clear by knowledge of the author. They are accepted not as authority but as giving additional information about the person. It seems immoral for critics to misuse this power to impose values—values related to something that perhaps was not even experienced and cannot be experienced.

Unlike teachers of, say, physics or mathematics, many teachers of academic courses in theatre spend most of their time teaching value judgments. The students are supposed to learn (or at least to agree) that the kind of theatre the teacher likes is really good and that the kind of theatre the teacher dislikes is really bad. If they learn this well, they pass the course. Because there is personal contact, the teacher-student relationship is more subtle and has more possibilities for qualification than does the critic-reader relationship, but in grading and recommendation the teacher has a greater direct power than does the critic. Teachers can force their values on others in ways that even critics cannot.

Another similarity between drama teachers and theatre critics is the amount of time/space devoted to interpretation. The discussion of values and meaning is a simple way to fill a class period. Just as everyone makes value responses, everyone senses meanings in events and in theatre, and most people who can speak at all well have no difficulty discussing themselves—their value judgments and interpretations—at some length. They are not "wrong," of course. But the teacher's values, opinions, and interpretations are no more "correct" than those of the students. The classroom situation is analogous in many ways to the situation of criticism. Both involve training in values.

Unfortunately for critics, no society (or readership) is completely homogeneous. There is constant pressure for those on either side of the norm to agree with the normative position. Thus, women, for example, have had to accept a critical value-structure normative to men. Is it an oversimplification to say that this is the main reason there have been no "great" women artists or "great" women playwrights? Isn't this pressure immoral? If critics (and teachers) refrained from making value judgments, it would not exist.

But let us put aside moral arguments. They can seem embarrassing, sentimental, and out-of-date in our age. Since they are subjective, they also come close to being value judgments themselves. Even though they function at a different level than do value judgments, and we could eliminate one while retaining the other, they can appeal only to an ethical "taste."

There is a fourth charge to be leveled against criticism. It is more direct and pragmatic than the moral one. Criticism as we know it is unnecessary and useless.

Published value judgments about theatre can be seen to have three possible functions. The first, which can be dismissed quickly, is that of the reviewer: indicating to potential spectators whether or not they would enjoy the performance. Such a service can be performed adequately without making value judgments. Many people seem to need only the names of the playwright, director, and/or leading actors. For many, a plot summary would be sufficient. Description and photographs would satisfy most. Some feel that the photographs posted outside of a movie theatre give an accurate forecast of the film. For those who need an evaluative recommendation, a rating in stars, asterisks, or some other symbol should be sufficient.

A second possible function of criticism is the creation and standardization of taste. There are critics who actually propose that they are establishing aesthetic standards. (Critics have already been accused of arrogance, and this is obvious arrogance. It implies that their standards are correct and are superior in some respect to the standards of others.) Even when no claims are made, the results are the same: the values of one person reinforce or contradict—thereby possibly changing—the values held by others. Individual taste is forced toward the norm or kept there.

If critics are speaking pseudo-objectively, they must be using value-indicating words in the way that they are generally understood by readers; they must be speaking to the norms of a particular society or sociological group. Thus, each reviewer can be seen as representing and speaking to a group that shares a common value system. He or she gains his position because of having the ability to reflect the values of a particular society. Success will depend upon how accurately the reviewer mirrors the taste of that audience. The *New York Times* reviewers are normative of the *Times* audience; the *Daily News* reviewers are normative of the *News* audience.

The fact that critics relate to the valuative norms of a society means that preexisting conditions and standards tend to determine and control criticism. Critics learn what has been thought to be "good" and "beautiful" in the past and pass these standards on to the future. This is excellent for preserving the status quo of a society, but it is not conducive to change. It stifles the development of new ideas and is a clear problem for avant-garde and experimental theatre. Standardization of taste is a repressive concept.

There are those teachers who say that they can tell their students which plays are good and which are bad because they have had more experience. They have seen more plays than any of their students, so their judgments are more accurate, better. Critics and reviewers, too, have seen many performances—more than most nontheatre people, more than almost any young person. Should those with more experience than they have be allowed to "correct" the taste of the teacher or critic just as they attempt to "correct" the taste of others? Should we all accept the standards of those who have the most experience and let their taste dictate to us all?

Nor is it possible to justify the establishment of critical standards as practical and functional. In certain societies, a fascism of taste is important, even vital, but there is no reason why any aesthetic standards should be imposed in a democracy. Under our democracy, the public evaluation of various religious beliefs—a practice that was once quite common—has now disappeared. This does not mean that everyone agrees about religious values. But religion, which was once debated openly, is no longer criticized in public. The mass media does not evaluate various theological beliefs. There is public freedom of religious values. The same should hold true for art, including the art of performance. Art, like religion, exists for the individual. Although both churches and theatres are public places, religion and art are personal and ultimately private experiences. There should be a public freedom of artistic values. There is no practical need for the public evaluation of theatre and the standardization of theatrical taste.

Some might claim that criticism has a historical function, that it serves as a record of our times. This is true, but the record is not valuable, irreplaceable, or necessary. Critical value judgments have no intrinsic historical importance. This does not mean that the critics of the past have no significance. Any historical artifact—including value judgment—can be useful to the historian. But the use is nonaesthetic. It may be sociopolitical, helping to trace patterns of taste and opinion. It may—like the value judgments of a diary—serve to typify the response of that period. It may be psychological, giving insight into the personality of the writer. (Psychological importance depends, of course, upon the historical importance of the person who recorded the statements of value. The taste of a famous person is historically significant. Some critics may hope to reverse the process and achieve historical importance merely because they are able to publish their value judgments while others are not.) Any record is sufficient for history; a critic's opinions do not need to be published and disseminated widely to be available to the historian. If critics completely ceased making value judgments, the future would be no poorer for it. Nothing would be lost that could not be obtained in other ways. Even the personal psychological data would be available if the critics merely wrote autobiographies or kept diaries.

Thus the public evaluation of art is unnecessary as well as being naive and primitive, arrogant, and immoral. It should be eliminated. The critic should refrain from making attributions of value. This would effectively do away with theatrical criticism as we know it. Should those who write about performance without evaluating it still be called "critics"? Should their value-free writings be referred to as "criticism"? It matters little, but the change in role might be clarified and emphasized by the use of new terms: We could speak of "performance analysts" who produce "performance documentation" and "performance analysis."

Although value judgments have no intrinsic historical importance, performance documentation and analysis does. Performance is ephemeral. It disappears from history unless it is recorded and preserved somehow. Thus a concern with history demands an accurate and objective record of the performance. To the extent that the record is complete and detailed, the performance can be reconstructed mentally. Values will take care of themselves. Since everyone has values, historical reconstruction will be evaluated. If people have accurate and exhaustive information, their evaluation will approximate the evaluation they would have made of the actual performance if they had been in the audience. But history does not care whether its data are liked or disliked; evaluation is built only on the quality and accuracy of the data.

Thus a fifth and final claim can be made against evaluative criticism: it tends to work against and obscure vital historical documentation. Each value judgment is based on some empirical observation, but an assertion of value is not the same as a description of what it was that gave rise to the feeling of value. Yet many critics objectify their taste, confuse description and evaluation, and substitute subjective feeling for objective detail. This prevents analysis by both the critic and the auditor/reader, who is left with insufficient data.

Criticism functions as a screen between the reader and historical fact. How much description is contained in the usual review? How much do we learn about the concert at Judson Church from reading Clive Barnes's review? Even when several or many reviews of the same production are available, one knows little or nothing about what actually took place on the stage. Critics other than reviewers seldom take the time or make the effort to describe performances. Historical fact has disappeared behind a screen of personal taste. For anyone interested in reconstructing historical productions, for anyone concerned with the history of performance rather than with the history of dramatic literature or taste, this is a serious problem. (For a case study of the problem, see the reviews of Antonin Artaud's 1935 production of *Les Cenci* collected in the *Drama Review,* June 1972. In addition to providing little information about the staging, they almost unanimously dismiss as a "bad" actor a figure of great historical importance—without describing his acting.)

When a difficult descriptive or analytical problem arises, the critic frequently resorts to a statement of value rather than attempting a description or analysis. It is not unfair to say that this is "the easy way." After all, everyone makes value judgments. But not everyone can describe significant detail or analyze theatrical relationships. It is much easier, for example, merely to characterize a particular performance as "good acting" or "bad acting" than it is to recognize and describe its particular, characteristic, and/or unique features or to analyze how it differs from other performances. Thus, positive or negative assertions of value by a critic frequently replace and prevent objective description and analysis. They frustrate historical need.

Some say that it is impossible to write about performance without making value judgments. "The very choice of a performance to be documented or analyzed," they say, "is a value judgment." That is not necessarily so. The choice may be based on a scientific claim that the data have significance of some sort. One does not need to like a performance to believe that it is significant. *The Fantasticks* had a certain sociological significance because of its long run; Grotowski's *The Constant Prince* had a certain significance as the embodiment of techniques and theories that have had a wide influence, and so on. Scientists are involved with their field. They care about it. They have preferences, likes, dislikes, hopes, fears. But they do not let their personal taste affect the objective nature of their work. Performance analysis also can take an objective and scientific approach. If it relates to value—even makes value the object of its analysis—it attempts to eliminate personal value from the selection, arrangement, and presentation of its material.

To repeat Santayana's quote, "beauty is a value . . . not a perception of a matter of fact or of a relation," the theatre analyst deals with matters of fact and with relationships rather than with values. If psychoanalysis is considered to be a science, performance analysis can be thought of in the same way. Yet, like psychoanalysis, it may not be able to eliminate all traces of value attribution. Conscious and intentional value judgment can be done away with, however. Analysts can refrain from obvious and explicit statements of value such as "the performances were excellent," "the writing was bad," "it was a beautiful piece," and so on. They can stop themselves from anthropomorphically claiming their own emotional response—or any personal response—to be a characteristic of the performance: "the impact was overwhelming," "it was a compelling work," "everything is infused with honesty and meaningfulness." Even to say that a piece "seems to have" characteristics of this kind refers to the effect on the critic and tells us nothing of the objective nature of the work.

If the performance analysts are careful, they can prevent conscious value judgments from entering their work. This is all that can be expected of them. They cannot be expected to control their unconscious. They may not realize that certain terminology conveys attributions of value. But they can attempt to make their presentations as free as possible from value judgments.

The elimination of intentional value judgment does not mean that subjectivity has been eliminated. Some will claim that, given the subjective nature of experience, one cannot be objective in the description of a performance. This is not true. If I say that there are three performers on stage, that one of them is a black girl, that none of them is speaking, and so forth, these statements are both value-free and objective. Certain objective facts can be established. They are independent of human desire and opinion.

Documentation does not need to omit personal response. How an audience reacts to a performance can be described objectively. It, too, is a historical fact. If the opinions of individuals are thought to be interesting or useful, they, too, can be reported; the "review" of the future could be a public opinion poll or a report on a controlled sample of predominantly "average" spectators. This egalitarian approach would replace today's elitist evaluations in which the taste of a single "authority" (or at least someone who can write clearly and expressively) establishes standards.

Of course, all assertions of fact do not have the same objectivity. To say that an actor is "tall" or a piece of scenery is "large" are attempts at objective description, but different people may have different standards of "tall" and "large." The important point is not that a certain element of subjectivity has entered, but that the words do not imply a value. "Tall" and "large" are neither good nor bad, beautiful nor ugly.

Even some words that are technical and impersonal are difficult to use without implying a value. They are "loaded." The words "primitive" and "naive," for example, tend to be taken as deprecatory, although there is not necessarily anything in their definition to establish this. Neither "primitive" nor "naive" is necessarily bad or good, but, unless they want to become involved in polemics, performance analysts should stay away from controversial and multivalent terminology. When they do use it, they should describe carefully the way they are employing the words and the standards that apply.

A problem could arise with those words that indicate both fact and value, that function both as objective description and indicators of personal response. To say that a play was "brilliant" might mean that it was brightly illuminated; it also could mean that it was exciting to someone. "Powerful" might indicate a high energy level—something that could be measured objectively by a machine—but it is also used to refer to a subjective response. Some people seem to use words of this kind in a perhaps unconscious attempt to give a spurious objectivity to their personal responses. The intent becomes clear, of course, from the context. There is no reason why ambiguity should exist, and a performance analyst can refrain from using these words in their evaluative sense.

To suggest that the criticism of art is useless and even harmful does not mean that all criticism should be abolished. Social and political criticism, for example, serves an important function. But its purpose is practical and pragmatic. It relates directly to the conditions of life. Art does not do this. It involves personal experience; its relationship to public life is indirect and cannot be predicted.

Some people use theatre for social and political criticism. Such explicit messages may certainly be criticized—but as social reform or politics rather than as art. The standards against which they are measured are pragmatic ones.

Even some artists confuse art and life. The accepted impracticality of art does not protect them from society's laws, however. The defacing of Picasso's *Guernica* painting at the Museum of Modern Art was defended as a work of conceptual art by an artist in a mimeographed letter calling for the kidnapping of museum trustees, directors, administrators, and curators to be held as "war hostages" until the arrested man was released. The Metropolitan Museum brought a charge of sending a kidnap threat through the mail. The letter was itself defended as a work of conceptual art, but it and the *Guernica* incident both show, by contrast, that most art has no practical consequences. When it does, it is a question of referral to the law rather than to criticism. Laws are necessary; critics are not.

To eliminate evaluation does not mean the end of discussion and debate. Science is objective, and yet the results of experiments and the validity and importance of scientific claims and theories are widely debated. Like scientific facts, theatrical facts may be incorrect. In a review published in the October 23, 1975, issue of the *New York Times,* Mel Gussow described Mabou Mines production of Samuel Beckett's *Come and Go.* The play, he said, "is staged in bright light in a space beneath the stage." This was factually incorrect. The actors were behind the spectators, who saw their reflections in a mirror placed in front of the raised stage. (Among other things, this gross but understandable error indicates again the problems of someone attempting to recreate historical productions from published material.) Analyses of theatre, theatrical theory, and ascriptions of importance are also open to challenge without resorting to value judgments.

To ask for the elimination of value judgments in criticism (and in the teaching of theatre) is an idealistic and utopian view. This does not mean that it is frivolous. It is intended seriously. Such a change in the nature of criticism as we know it may eventually take place. It may be as frowned upon then publicly to evaluate another's aesthetic values as it is now publicly to evaluate another's religious preferences. That future will be a more efficient, a more moral, and, to many, a more satisfying time in which to live.

chapter six

the question of efficacy

Many people believe that theatre—and all art—must have efficacy in the everyday world. They think theatre should change what people think and the way they act. Theatre that does not attempt to do this is merely entertainment.

Political theatre is certainly a clear example of performance that attempts to make practical changes in the society. If we were constructing a continuum against which to measure degrees of social efficacy—at least intended efficacy—we could place most political theatre at one end of the scale, the "high" end. In this sense, political theatre can be seen to represent all theatre in its search for efficacy. Let us examine political theatre and analyze its ability to change society.

There are those who say that all theatre is political. To a great extent, this is a semantic problem. Their view is frequently based upon a misunderstanding of the word "political." Webster defines "political" as:

1. of or concerned with government, the state, or politics.
2. having a definite governmental organization.
3. engaged in or taking sides in politics; as *political* parties.
4. of or characteristic of political parties or politicians: as *political* pressure.

These definitions may help us understand the nature of political theatre, but they do not apply to all theatrical activity.

Some of the people who claim that all theatre is political seem to confuse "political," "social," and "economic." Of course, all theatre exists in a certain socioeconomic context. By definition, it involves an audience; it is not a solitary activity. But this does not mean that it necessarily is concerned with government or that it must take sides in politics. The psychological elements and interpersonal relationships of, say, *A Streetcar Named Desire* may be magnified into social statements. Blanche may become in someone's mind the representative of a social class. But this does not give us a play "of or concerned with government." If *The Lower*

Depths were a political indictment, it would not have been performed under the czarist government. Most plays make no political statement.

Indeed, a basic functional independence of theatre and politics can be illustrated by certain indigenous performances that have remained unchanged for many years under various political parties, systems, and orders. Although government and politics may be useful to human beings as social animals, they are not inevitable or always necessary. Many activities—a couple making love, a card game among friends, a doctor performing an operation—are not inherently related to politics. There is no reason why theatre should be.

Webster's definitions of "political" stress active intent. Theatre is political if it is *concerned with* the state or *takes sides* in politics. This allows us to define "political theatre" in a way that distinguishes it from other kinds of theatre: it is a performance that is intentionally concerned with government, that is intentionally engaged in or consciously takes sides in politics. Although intentionality is a subjective state, there is no problem in using it as a defining factor. Communication is, of course, imperfect. Artists may not achieve all their specific, subtle, and half-conscious goals, but their intent is not likely to be misunderstood. If a theatre piece is intended to be political and the intent is not perceived, there is no need to categorize it as "political theatre." Thus, if a presentation does not attempt to be political, it is not political.

Of course, certain situations and certain governments may force all theatre to be political. It can be an external rather than an internal decision. Censorship is a good example of this. By passing laws about theatre, a government may create a relationship between itself and all performance. But a performance is political—it is "of" the government—only as it relates to such laws. Generally, theatre is political only to the extent that it attempts to be political. Most theatre has no concern for or interest in politics.

Political theatre does not merely deal with government as a passive subject. It makes explicit reference to contemporary government problems and issues. Thus, *Oedipus* and *Hamlet* are not political plays merely because their protagonists are sovereigns. Hypothetically, of course, any script can be given a political production; on the other hand, a political script may lose its dynamic political quality with the passing of time. An antiwar play like Sheriff's *Journey's End* was not political—although it could be considered moralistic—when it was produced in New York in the 1928–29 season.

Some people, however, are able to relate any performance to the government or the state in their own minds. They interpret theatre politically.

Such interpretation depends upon the person doing the interpretation; it is not inherent in the work. Any belief system—a religion, a social or psychological schema—may be projected onto a presentation. For example, anything created by man can be interpreted according to Freud's concepts as a revelation of the unconscious. Would it be helpful or useful, then, if we referred to all drama as "psychoanalytical theatre"? Because something may somehow and to some extent be interpreted as being political does not mean that it is political. In the Rorschach tests even an inkblot formed by chance produces many interpretations. Political concern and engagement must be in the work, not in the mind of the observer.

As with any interpretive system, the political interpretation of performance depends upon the political knowledge of the interpreter. But political knowledge is not theatre knowledge. Many interpreters of theatre know a lot about their own area of intellectual concern but little about performance. They relate everything they perceive to intellectual standards and structures that exist entirely apart from theatre. If all theatre ceased to exist, these political patterns of thought would be unchanged.

Italian Futurism has suffered greatly at the hands of those who interpret everything politically. Its accomplishments in performance have been denigrated, rejected, and suppressed because certain of its members—including its leader, Filippo Tommaso Marinetti—were politically active in support of Fascism. But other Futurists had no political involvement. Futurism was not a political movement. Very few of the plays contained explicitly political statements or supported a particular political position.

To those who are intent on distorting art into politics, however, explicit political intent is not necessary. Thus it is claimed that it was the spirit of Italian Futurism that was fascistic. Yet Italian Futurism spread almost immediately to Russia, where it joined forces with the proletarian revolution. The same Futurist spirit imbued artists who held opposite political views.

The Futurists are also deprecated by some political thinkers because both they and the Nazis were influenced by Friedrich Nietzsche. Guilt by association is an old tool of political thought. Of course, an American—or a Chinese—can reject Italian Fascism, Russian Communism, and Nazism along with Nietzsche, but this is not theatrical thought or analysis. The same artistic philosophy can relate to opposing political positions. On the other hand, can anyone point out a form or style of theatre—any artistic element at all—that can be used by only one political position or ideology?

One mental mechanism that the political interpreter uses to make all theatre political is either/or thinking. A performance is either for a certain political position or it is against it. Thus all theatre apparently is forced to be political. As the slogan of the late 1960s said: "You are either part of the solution, or you are part of the problem." Of course, this thinking is simple-minded. It is similar to "Have you stopped beating your wife?" A logical formulation can produce its own answer. If one has to think in either/or terms, it could be said that theatre is either political or it is not political.

Some feel that all experimental and avant-garde theatre is political because it is different than—and therefore opposed to—the traditional and accepted. Any theatre that is radical artistically is considered to be radical politically. Since the government in power is part of and supported by the status quo, any variation from the status quo is seen as a threat to and an attack upon that government. When talking about his ideal state in *The Republic,* Plato said: "This is the point to which, above all, the attention of our rulers should be directed: that music and gymnastics be preserved in their original form and no innovation be made . . . any musical innovation is full of danger to the whole State and ought to be prohibited . . . [because] when modes of music change, the fundamental laws of the State always change with them."

Art does change the way people think, and new ways of thinking may eventually cause changes in laws and government. But this does not justify calling all theatre political. Political theatre is explicit in pointing out the institutions and aspects of government that should change; it often describes and supports the exact nature of these changes. Nobody knows how art, with its indirect causality, will change the world. Nobody can predict its effects. If art causes change, it is not necessarily political change.

Let us take a specific example and see how political interpretation generally works. Richard Foreman is presenting *Sophia=(Wisdom) Part 3: The Cliffs* in the SoHo district of New York. The characters are not represented in a particular social environment and there is no reference to or indication of political subject matter and intent. Of course, the interpreter may claim that the play is opposed to his chosen political position since it is not for it, but the same simplistic reasoning could be used by a socialist, a democrat, or an anarchist.

Given no intellectual message to analyze, however, political interpreters will not get very far. Usually, they will not be interested in such a performance. They will ignore messageless theatre because it gives them little to work with according to their system. If forced to deal with abstract and nonreferential works, political interpreters will turn their attention to the makeup of the company, to the audience, and to the social context of the piece. They will find out, for example, that the actors are college educated, that they earn little from their performance, and that the production is supported by a grant. The spectators, an analyst will find, are entirely middle, upper-middle, and upper class; some are artists, many are under thirty, all are knowledgeable in theatre. This special and identifiable audience can then be placed in the larger social context. It can be compared to the society at large and recognized as a functional subgroup.

This much is sociology. It is the sociology of theatre but sociology nonetheless. As a pure scientist, the sociologist would stop at this point. He or she would gather the facts, analyze them, and organize them. He would not say that the facts are good or bad, right or wrong. The political interpreter goes further. He sets up political standards within which the facts may be evaluated and criticized. He claims, of course, that these standards are objectively true and that the political values he deduces from them are inherent in the work. Thus, he might say that Foreman's *Sophia* is politically wrong because it does not cater to the masses of the proletariat (who are "good") and that, being "aristocratic" and "elitist" the performance is evil. Thus, political values and standards have been imposed on the work. They say nothing about the presentation as theatre and as art.

This example illustrates how a political view of theatre is intellectual. It does not deal with theatre as a personal, sensory (as well as mental) experience. The real, individual experience of the performance does not matter in this approach. Personal sensations have no social or political aspect. Like the sociologist (rather than the psychologist), the political interpreter deals only with symbolic information and social data; unlike the sociologist, he refers them for evaluation to a political system of thought. The experience of theatre has been avoided for the sake of political intellectualization. This intellectualization has its own emotional base, but it is imposed on the work rather than being intended by it.

The view that all theatre is political ignores a study of theatre in favor of a study of politics. In criticism, then, a work becomes good or bad to the extent that it agrees with or opposes the observer's own political position. Since people who do and are interested in political theatre tend to be liberal, it is impossible, for example, to have a "good" play that supports a conservative administration or its policies. Political standards replace theatrical ones.

In theatrical terms, one content or message is not better or worse than another. Theatre analysts are concerned with the way content—whatever that content might be—relates to particular theatrical devices and techniques. They are concerned with the functional relationships between style and expression, between performance and audience. It is important to study and analyze political theatre not because of and in terms of its politics but because it illustrates and illuminates particular theatrical dimensions.

Thus political performances, presentations that make explicit reference to political issues and conditions, can be seen as examples of strongly referential theatre. Their reference, their "aboutness"—what they are about and what they say about the subject—is usually quite clear.

Another aspect of political theatre, quite apart from its reference, is its attempt, in almost every case, to change the opinions and beliefs of the spectator. This can be done in many different ways, ranging from the most overt and explicit to the most covert and hidden. Thus it would be possible to place any political production at some point along a conversion continuum depending on the means and techniques that it employed. At one end would be pieces that involved direct argumentation and aggressive propaganda; at the other end would be pieces that sought to achieve an attitude change through what could be called seduction. Many nonpolitical performances would also find a place on this continuum. (I am not referring here to therapeutic forms such as psychodrama and prison workshops in which theatre techniques are used to change the personalities of the participants but to didactic theatre directed toward the audience.)

Most political theatre, rather than merely posing political questions and problems, attempts to change the beliefs and opinions of the spectator. Ultimately, it seeks political action based on these changes. In *Notes of a Director*, Alexander Tairov describes what could be called an archetypal example of political theatre, an incident that crystallizes the deep ambitions of those who seek to use theatre for political ends:

In 1830, at the Théâtre Monnaie in Brussels, the play *La Muette* was being performed. In the middle of the performance, when the words "Love for the Fatherland is holy" rang out on the stage, the revolutionary enthusiasm . . . was communicated to the auditorium. The whole theatre was united in such powerful transport that all the spectators and actors left their places, grabbing chairs, benches—everything that came to hand—and, bursting from the theatre, rushed into the streets of Brussels. Thus, began the Belgian revolution.

On the other hand, the political realities of theatre often do not coincide with the realities of everyday life. Enrique Buenaventura, the director of Colombia's Teatro Experimental de Cali, has described in a mimeographed handout an incident that can be seen to characterize political theatre in a way that is practical rather than archetypal:

> There are groups in Colombia . . . who are, we say back home, very "acceler-ated." They like to travel light. Some of these people put on a play in which they were both soldiers and guerrillas. The guerrillas . . . had a discussion with the soldiers, they convinced the soldiers, and the soldiers changed over to the side of the guerrillas because they *understood the problem*. The play ended with everyone giving the clenched fist salute of solidarity. A few days after the show, the army occupied the theatre and the School of Fine Arts using real rifles. During the occupation, I went over to the actors who had been in the play and asked them, "Why don't you go over to the soldiers and speak with them, and see if you can convince them?" And they didn't go because they knew the soldiers would hit them over the head.

Thus it is worthwhile to consider pragmatically the actual effective-ness of political theatre—and, by inference, of all didactic theatre. To what extent is theatre able to change beliefs and opinions? What are the obstacles to achieving these changes? What are the factors that relate to the political effectiveness of theatre? Few conclusive answers are avail-able, but certain hypotheses may be presented.

One important consideration is the effectiveness of live theatre as compared to other means of communication. Is it more or less effective than, say, television or film? In a symposium at the American Place The-atre, John Houseman ascribed a "seminal effect" to theatre. He appar-ently felt that, although the theatre audience was relatively small, the impact of theatre as a medium was somehow greater and more power-ful than that of other media. He did not explain how this is true, how-ever, and until there are data to show that live performance actually is more compelling intellectually and more able to change opinion and be-lief, we are able to say only that the experience of theatre is different from that of other media. Arguing logically from these differences, one might say that the actual presence of the actor increases the reality of the experience, making it more potent. The "live" quality of a performance may be thought to give it more political efficacy than the same perfor-mance would have on film.

On the other hand, television, film, and even radio can be seen to have a greater power to make the unreal seem real. Thousands of people actually believed Orson Welles's "War of the Worlds" broadcast and acted accordingly. Some fled their homes; some prepared to defend themselves against the Martian invaders. It would be possible to use staged news footage on television without anyone realizing that it was not, in fact, real. Thus, live theatre tends to retain an "editorializing" dimension; the commentator and the comments almost always remain separate and distinct. When this is true, political theatre may be seen as being more limited than other media in changing opinion and belief. During the same American Place symposium, former Senator Eugene McCarthy said that because of his appearance on television Walter Cronkite was the "most trusted man in America." Theatre, on the other hand, is recognized—and appreciated—for its "lies."

As suggested by the reference to Cronkite, the size of the audience—both in absolute numbers and in the frequency with which an individual spectator is contacted—may be seen as relevant to effectiveness. If success is measured by the number of people whose opinions or beliefs are changed, it might be assumed that a presentation of any efficacy at all will have success directly proportional to the size of its audience. Obviously, live theatre, because of the practical limitations of the medium, does not reach as large an audience as does film and television. The Ford Foundation study *The Finances in the Performing Arts* reports that "71 percent of the people [a sample of six thousand in twelve major cities] saw a movie on television more than once a month, and 41 percent more than once a week, but hardly any people saw a live professional performance of a play more than once a month." Nor do spectators tend to see the same live performers over and over, as they are apt, for example, to do on television serials. This, apparently, is one reason why Jerzy Grotowski opened rehearsals to the public; because they present relatively few works, even a regional or community theatre does not have the same following as, say, a local softball team. In these conditions, the believability of the commentator/actor remains minimal.

Of course, absolute numbers and frequency of contact are not the only audience factors related to effectiveness. The composition of the audience that is reached is also important. If one wishes to change someone's beliefs and opinions, it is necessary to contact those who do not already agree. No change will take place if political theatre is performed only for spectators who think the same as the writer/director/performers.

This is one of the major problems that has faced political theatre: how to find or attract the audience that can be converted. It is the basis for guerrilla theatre, which takes its performances to audiences that never planned to see the particular play but find it thrust upon them in one way or another, and it explains why many political theatre groups depend upon humor to a great extent.

Once the proper audience—the audience that does not already agree—has been found, the second problem arises: making the spectators listen to and accept what is said. Intellectual resistance may be encountered. There is a natural tendency for spectators to react *against* anything that does not conform with their existing beliefs.

This is not merely a question of antagonism. It is true that certain political groups in the United States in the late 1960s actually antagonized their audiences in the belief that they could, in this way, persuade them. But when passersby were splashed with "blood" by a guerrilla theatre troupe performing an antiwar skit in the street, they tended to get angry rather than become enlightened. The belligerent and self-concerned attitude of the Living Theatre in *Paradise Now* offended and alienated many who were sympathetic to the intellectual aims of the group. When a theatre tells its audience, "I am right; you are wrong," most spectators will intellectually support and elaborate their own position. An attack causes not surrender, but defense. If this psychological generality is true, it brings into question the efficacy of much political theatre.

Perhaps an attack is not seen as an attack. There is the story, perhaps apocryphal, of the general who attended *Oh, What a Lovely War*, Joan Littlewood's antiwar—and antimilitary—production. He thought it was wonderful and said he enjoyed it more than any play he had ever seen. Years before, Rousseau had explained the psychology behind such incidents. In *Politics and the Arts*, he wrote:

> In the quarrels at which we are purely spectators, we immediately take the side of justice, and there is no act of viciousness which does not give us a lively sentiment of indignation so long as we receive no profit from it. But when our interest is involved, our sentiments are soon corrupted. And it is only then that we prefer the evil which is useful to us to the good that nature makes us love.

The goal of most political theatre is to reach an audience of the masses, an audience of working people, an audience of the common man. Since theatre people do not see themselves as belonging to this class—and, indeed, most political theatre has been produced by educated people from the middle class and above—and since the masses are conceived as uneducated, perhaps quasi-literate, and of low intelligence, many political plays intentionally use childish, crude, or simple techniques and thought. This creates an "us versus them" feeling that does not exist in most theatre. It also can seem condescending. It is possible, however, for a spectator to identify with the intelligent "us" rather than the unintelligent "them" and to gain a sense of superiority.

A similar mechanism is behind a much wider spectrum of theatre. All referential theatre that attempts to send a message to the masses—not merely political theatre but the theatre of moral uplift and the Great American Play—functions on the same us/them basis. Those who write the play, or perhaps merely those who back it and approve it, think that they know what is right and wrong with the country and what the country should think and believe. The great play they seek is the one that tells the masses what they themselves, the seekers, already know. Most of these people probably wonder why we do not have a Great American Play and mourn the state of our theatre.

Joseph Papp is one of those who think in terms of "meaningful" plays, "ones that address themselves to the major psychological problems of our time." Of course, it is Papp who knows what is meaningful, to whom it should be meaningful, and what our important problems are. Emphasis on this theatre-as-education given by an informed or enlightened teacher to an uninformed or unenlightened public can be traced back at least to Horace. It is one of the main supports of political theatre.

Certainly political theatre has to be judged ineffective when compared with the political actions of everyday life. Terrorism is sometimes a very effective means of achieving practical goals. It is used to call attention to a particular cause, to raise large amounts of money very quickly, to force the release of prisoners, and so forth. In comparison, theatre is relatively or completely inefficient. Traditional political means are also more effective than theatre. If this were not so, we would have fewer speeches by politicians in this country, and the political parties would be supporting extensive theatrical activity.

If political theatre, when compared to other political means, is seen as relatively inefficient, there are certain pragmatic indicators that would suggest the same conclusion. In retrospect, the great surge of anti–Vietnam War theatre can be seen as a small part of the general political activism of the period. Like the activism, its rather sudden decline took place long before the withdrawal of American troops from Vietnam. It reached its peak at the time of the shooting at Kent State in May 1970, and by the time the bombing raids on North Vietnam were intensified in 1972, political theatre activity was almost nonexistent. It was a fashion, so to speak. Apparently the practitioners of political theatre found it to be useless. Most did not give up theatre, they merely gave up theatre that dealt explicitly with current issues. Such issues still exist, but almost all political theatre in the United States prefers to deal with general, theoretical questions where the success or failure in changing a spectator's beliefs and opinions is not apparent. Earlier, Erwin Piscator, a leading exponent of this form of theatre—his book is entitled *Political Theatre*—fared no better. He was successful neither financially nor politically.

It would be wrong, however, to consider the effectiveness of political theatre only in terms of changing the beliefs and opinions of the spectators. Some political theatre does not do this. It merely raises certain issues, explores certain problems, asks certain questions. It does not proselytize, it is not didactic, it does not support particular alternatives.

Nor is the changing of beliefs and opinions the only possible practical result of political theatre. If, especially when compared with other political tools, theatre can be seen to have little power to change a spectator's position, its impact can still be significant. It can give emotional and intellectual support to those who already agree with its position. Just as a marching band helps to stir the soldier's patriotism, courage, and fighting spirit, political theatre can be the rallying point for the believers in a particular cause. It can give them the feeling that they are not alone in their beliefs, that others are actively involved and pursuing the same goals. Thus it can be an important force in political change.

We have been considering efficacy in terms of a model that consciously attempts to create social change directly. There is another model—the model of indirect and nonintentional change. Although intentionality, of course, has a great deal to do with the characteristics of the theatre being created, it has no necessary relation to efficiency. A piece may intend to be socially efficacious and achieve nothing; theatre that has no intention of bringing about change may actually do so. Social change is a subtle and complex phenomenon. It does not always take place in the context of intellectual ideas, communication, and didacticism.

Theatre may change society indirectly. Any theatre that is "up-to-date" and "in style" creates change by participating in the broad waves of fashion and taste that continue—at least in our society—both to mirror and to alter people's behavior and their view of the world. When I discussed perceptual states in chapter 4, I was referring not to *what* is perceived but to the *way* in which the world is perceived. If theatre can change, in any way at all, the manner in which people see the world, the thoughts, actions, and behavior of these people will change. The way the behavior will change is not explicit in the performance, however. It is not dictated or prescribed by the theatrical work. It is indirect, rather than direct, change.

To change society in an indirect (or even direct) way, it is not necessary to reach a large number of people. Most of the practical and functional changes in society are caused by relatively few people. Social change comes almost entirely from intellectuals: scientists, technicians, teachers, lawyers, politicians, and the like. If these people's perceptions of the world are changed, social change of some sort will result. Because the world of art and, to a somewhat lesser extent, theatre is so closely involved with the intelligentsia, it is in a favorable position to effect indirect change. Unlike political theatre workers who feel they must go to a different social class for their audience, the audience for theatre as art belongs to the same general social group as the the theatre artists. The dissemination of ideas of this kind occurs to a great extent through the specialized journals of the intelligentsia rather than through the mass media.

We may posit, for example, that Freud's theories of the symbolic interpretation of dreams and of everyday life would not have been developed if it had not been for the art movement known as Symbolism. Symbolism is a system, a way of perceiving the world. Although that system involves content, it is independent of any particular content. Symbolist art predated Freud. It saturated the intellectual life of Vienna, where Freud lived. It created a way of looking at the world that produced Freud's theories.

That is how the indirect influence of art and theatre on society progresses—not immediately, through many people, but by diffusion from the few to the many. This is not an elitist concept. It does not imply that the intellectual or creator is better than the worker or housewife. It does suggest that they are different and that theatre should be aware of these differences. It means that the theatre we should look to as the progenitor of social change is not a theatre of the masses, a theatre of entertainment and education, but a specialized theatre that investigates, among other things, the possibilities of perception and of the mind.

Possibilities are not negative. The opening of one possibility does not close other possibilities. In these terms, innovation is important in itself. Knowing and being able to predict exactly what changes will result from it is not particularly important. There is an efficacy, if an indirect one, in the new.

avant-garde theatre

Many years ago, I overheard a sailor who had traveled all over the world telling a story. One evening in some foreign port—let's say that it was in China—he happened to meet a young woman. After conversing for a while in what we may imagine to be pidgin English, the sailor was invited by the woman to her room. Happily, he went with her. As he was undressing, however, he heard someone laugh; it was not the young woman. Examining the room, the sailor found that people were watching them through small holes drilled in the walls.

Was this avant-garde theatre? The unusual spectator-performance relationship and the use of one, let us say, "untrained" performer relate it strongly to certain avant-garde performances. The avant-garde cannot be defined in terms of objective style and characteristics, however. Once available, styles and characteristics may be borrowed and used by anyone; this does not mean that they are still avant-garde.

Nevertheless, the performance seems innovative in an absolute sense. It is different from almost any other theatre we know. Can't the avant-garde be defined in terms of innovation? No, not all innovation belongs to the avant-garde. We tend to describe any theatre artist—actor, director, writer, and so forth—in terms of his or her unique and unusual contributions and personal innovations. Mainstream theatre, too, puts a price on innovation.

This search for the reasons why the strange performance described by the sailor was not avant-garde will lead us to two conceptual models of avant-garde theatre. These models will, in turn, be helpful in explaining recent changes and developments in avant-garde performance. To understand the nature of the avant-garde, let us look at its origins.

Some people point to the first production of Alfred Jarry's *Ubu Roi* in 1896 in Paris as the beginning of avant-garde theatre. Even before the performance began, Jarry had offended the taste of many of the spectators. He gave the traditional opening speech with his face painted white and spoke on only two notes—in his usual, but assumed, voice. Instead of the traditional white cloth, the table that held the water pitcher and glass was covered with a coal sack. When the first word of the play itself was spoken—"*merde*" ("shit"), slightly modified to "*merdre*" but still completely intelligible—a battle ensued in the auditorium. According to one report, the actor playing the part of Ubu improvised a wild dance for fifteen minutes until the clamor subsided enough for the play to continue. Thus *Ubu Roi* became the origin of an avant-garde theatre that intentionally attacks traditional taste. This is the mode of "*épater la bourgeoisie*"—literally, "startle the middle class." It can be followed through Futurism, Dada, and Surrealism. The Futurists and Dadaists intentionally provoked the spectators into violent attacks. The Surrealists attended bourgeois dramas (and some that were not bourgeois) so as to heckle and disrupt them from the auditorium. We can call this the "antagonistic" model of avant-garde theatre.

If the model is taken literally, however, little theatre in the last half-century can be found to fit it. Certainly, performances today do not cause battles. Walking out of a play before it is over is usually the most aggressive action taken by spectators, and this happens in all kinds of theatre, generally provoked more by boredom than by anger.

I have attended quite a lot of theatre, particularly avant-garde theatre, and I have seen only one overt confrontation by the bourgeoisie. At the Nancy Festival in 1973, I should have suspected something unusual was going on when, as I stood talking outside one of the administration tents, a poster advertising a performance by Frank Gallo was suddenly and violently ripped down by a passerby, who quickly disappeared. I did not suspect anything, however, and was not prepared for what happened the next evening at the opening performance of Gallo's *Squalls*. *Squalls* was presented in the intimate Italianate opera house that faces the main square in Nancy. The auditorium had large, well-padded seats and had been recently painted and decorated. Even as I found my place—fortunately, as it turned out, to one side—many of the spectators were making loud, belligerent comments. When the performance began, so did the physical assault. Vegetables flew through the air. From one of the boxes near the stage, someone attempted to throw a bucket of water down on the performers; he lost his grip, and the bucket almost hit one of the actors. Then some people who had gotten into the orchestra pit managed to turn on one of the emergency fire hoses. They sprayed the stage with a powerful stream of water. The performance was stopped briefly so the water could be cleared away. The verbal assault went on.

Obviously, it was not the performance itself that antagonized and infuriated a certain part of the audience. As with *Ubu Roi* and the even earlier famous battle at the opening of *Hernani,* spectators came prepared to fight. (This earlier battle was over the rules of playwriting rather than more general aesthetic concerns. The avant-garde had not yet developed.) But both Jarry's and Victor Hugo's scripts had been published; Gallo's performance probably did not have a script in the usual sense. What was it that had so disturbed some of the inhabitants of Nancy? Frank Gallo is gay. During the preparation of *Squalls,* he seemed to flaunt the fact. He was seen frequently around Nancy wearing fanciful, revealing, and unusual leather and plastic clothing. It was apparently this personal image and the way of life it suggested that not only offended many people but provoked them to the violent protest in the theatre. If the performance had been in Paris, a much more cosmopolitan city, the same thing might not have happened. Yet according to the model of *Ubu Roi,* this was the only avant-garde performance I have ever seen.

It is clear that we need to alter the model. Fluxus, a neo-Dada group of the early 1960s, performed mostly in lofts for audiences of friends and other knowledgeable art world people. The audience understood that it was not they who were being attacked, and they were not offended. They viewed the work in an aesthetic context. In an attempt to reach the proper audience, or at least a wider one, George Maciunas, the founder of Fluxus, rented the Carnegie Recital Hall on 57th Street in Manhattan. Unfortunately, it was still an art world audience that attended. There was, however, a group of three or four young couples in the balcony. Apparently they had been out together with nothing particular to do and had seen the formal photograph of the Flux Orchestra in tuxedos outside the theatre. The "musicians" indeed looked like members of a symphony orchestra. Expecting a concert of music, the young people watched the musicians raise and lower their hats as they followed a piano-roll score; they saw a rubber glove appear from the bell of a trombone; and so forth. Deeply disturbed, it seemed, they left—with no physical protest. The friends of Fluxus stayed on.

Thus we have a more detailed model for the antagonistic avant-garde. It includes an audience with particular antibourgeois or nonbourgeois tastes that senses the bourgeoisie would be offended *if* they were present. Shared awareness of potential insult becomes a positive value in the performance.

The voyeuristic theatre described in the sailor's story might seem to fit this model well. It certainly was not to the taste of the bourgeoisie. They would have been offended if they had been there. Like the sympathetic spectators at the Fluxus concerts, the voyeurs shared common values and expectations about the performance. Still, we cannot accept it as avant-garde. Aesthetics are lacking. The performance did not place itself in the context of art. It did not embody a particular art attitude, and the spectators, however unified in their taste, did not see it as art. That nameless city in what we have taken to be China probably did not even have an avant-garde. Not all countries—and relatively few cities in those countries—do. The avant-garde is a sociocultural phenomenon that does not exist everywhere. It is the product of a relatively small subgroup within that minority portion of the population that is involved with and cares about art.

Indeed, this is the historical background of the avant-garde. It did not always exist. It is a relatively new phenomenon, developing in the latter half of the nineteenth century. It did not begin—it could not begin—until the intellectual and artistic classes had grown (along with the total population) to a point at which it was possible to have a smaller, specialized art world within (or beside) the general art world. This specialized social grouping was devoted to the tastes of the artists themselves and to those of the educated people who knew and cared about art. In part, it revolved around artists' clubs and semiprivate cabarets. It did not direct its work to the general public or to the traditional taste of the established ruling class. A small subgroup of society began to direct its work toward itself.

This view of the avant-garde describes the socioaesthetic context within which a certain art form develops. That art may or may not reach a different and wider social group; it may or may not become popular and/or commercial. Whether it does or not, it remains avant-garde. Historically, avant-garde performance has reached a wide public to varying degrees. Dada was seen by relatively few. Expressionism, in its somewhat popularized form, briefly became part of the "mainstream" in Germany. Some avant-garde theatre people have gone on to successful careers outside the avant-garde; others have not. Antoine directed at the Odeon. The poet Paul Fort closed the Theatre d'Art after two years and never worked in theatre again. (This does not mean, of course, that art influenced by the avant-garde is also avant-garde. The Blue Blouse took Futurist machine dances and other avant-garde techniques to the masses without itself being avant-garde. Nor is everything necessarily avant-garde that is done by a previously avant-garde artist. Antoine's work at the Odeon was no longer avant-garde.)

Avant-garde theatre began—before that first performance of *Ubu Roi*—at least with the Symbolists. Symbolist aesthetics demonstrate a turning inward, away from the bourgeois world and its standards, to a more personal, private, and extraordinary world. Symbolist performance was done in small theatres. It was detached, distant, and static, involving little physical energy. The lighting was often dim. The actors often worked behind scrims; they were motionless for long periods and spoke in monotones. The subject matter of Symbolist plays was often religious. Roinard's *The Song of Songs* was based on passages from the Bible; the protagonist of Quillard's *The Girl With Cut-Off Hands* had her severed limbs miraculously restored through prayer. (Both pieces were staged at the Théâtre d'Art in Paris in 1891.) There was no confrontation of the bourgeoisie, no satire, no attack on anyone else's values or standards. The bourgeois world simply did not exist, even as a contrast conception. The art was self-contained, isolated, complete in itself. We can call this the "hermetic" model of avant-garde performance.

To the extent, of course, that hermetic avant-garde work is different from other art, it is apt to cause those who appreciate the other work to become defensive and antagonistic. Thus any innovative work might be shocking to someone who has only the most general, most popular, most widely held view of art. It has not been the intent, however, of all avant-garde artists to shock the public. Not all avant-garde work intends to deny, subvert, or confront traditional mainstream values. Many avant-garde artists direct their work toward a specialized audience whose values, standards, and concerns are quite different from those of the general public. It is not the bourgeoisie with which this hermetic avant-garde is concerned.

The tradition of *épater la bourgeoisie* explains only one aspect of the avant-garde. It would be impossible to trace a complete history of avant-garde theatre (or of avant-garde art in general) using only the antagonistic model. Much aesthetically radical performance, ranging from Symbolism to Bauhaus formalism, simply would not fit. We need two models—both the antagonistic and the hermetic—to explain the avant-garde. They will also help us analyze certain recent developments in avant-garde performance.

One often hears that the avant-garde is dead. Is this true? Certainly there is no sociological necessity for an avant-garde to exist. Because it is a product of a refined and self-conscious sociopsychological historical development, it has never existed in many cultures. It has been eliminated, or almost so, by certain political regimes in particular countries. But there seems to be no sociological reason why the avant-garde should have disappeared from the United States in the last decade.

Let us look at recent history and the contemporary situation using our two models of the avant-garde. During the 1960s, the antagonistic mode was dominant. Some performances attempted not merely to change the values of the bourgeoisie but to bring about actual social changes. The Living Theatre tried—usually with very little success—to turn *Paradise Now* into a street demonstration that would, for example, free prisoners from a nearby prison. Other work clashed with the legally formalized taste of the bourgeoisie. The producers of a play called *Che!* went on trial in New York for putting (simulated but partly concealed and therefore convincing) sexual intercourse on stage. *Dionysus in '69* by the Performance Group used nudity that was shocking enough to middle-class taste, at least in Michigan when the play was performed there, to cause legal action and prohibition of the presentation. If there was little actual confrontation in the theatres themselves, there was a raw, abrasive style and an aggressive or pugnacious attitude in many productions. Off-Off-Broadway plays frequently used intentionally vulgar remarks and the obscenities that were (and are) considered tasteless by the bourgeoisie.

This avant-garde theatrical activity certainly has diminished and seems to be extinct. Many of the well-known and successful groups in New York disbanded as their success began to fade. The Bread and Puppet Theatre moved to Vermont, although the group still reappears somewhat regularly to perform nonconfrontational theatre in the city. The Living Theatre is in unwanted exile in Italy (where its radical politics have found backing) because its members cannot support themselves financially in New York.

During the 1960s, there was a strong liberal tendency in the United States of which the marked difference of opinion about the advisability of conducting a war in Vietnam was just one aspect. Any anticonventional and/or antiestablishment manifestation tended to draw a supportive audience. This attitude was independent of any particular performance. As with the negative attitude toward Frank Gallo manifested at the performance of *Squalls,* this positive energy existed *before* a performance began. It was not a reaction to it.

There has, of course, been a great swing in the general public during the last decade from the political left toward the political right. The country in general, and New York with it, has become much more conservative. The defeat of the Equal Rights Amendment and the reelection of President Ronald Reagan are merely two obvious symptoms of this tendency. In theatre, one symptom is the tendency toward nostalgia and the revival of older plays. (Nostalgia is the opposite of the avant-garde attitude. It opposes a yearning for the safe, remembered values of the past to an orientation toward new values and toward the future.) There is the attempt to find a new "great playwright" (or one enough people can agree is really good) to continue the pre-1960s literary tradition. People who were once interested in avant-garde work suggest that the only theatre worth seeing can be found on Broadway, and so on. When a widespread, radical, nonconformist, antiestablishment attitude disappeared, interest in an antagonistic avant-garde disappeared with it. Does this mean that avant-garde theatre itself is dead?

Because it fit so well the tone of the times, the antagonistic avant-garde of the 1960s received wide attention in the media—even from those who had not seen it, did not like it, and/or did not agree with its implications. A certain sensationalism helped. It may be that the lack of media coverage and the absence of a recent international "superstar" leads one to suppose the avant-garde is dead. (Richard Foreman and Robert Wilson, the United States superstars of the 1970s, are, after all, still working.) Perhaps the avant-garde cannot be considered to be alive without a newly found representative in the international spotlight.

There is a new, international, U.S. superstar, however. In 1983, Laurie Anderson presented her *United States: Parts I–IV* to sold-out houses and standing ovations at the Brooklyn Academy of Music and was profiled in the Sunday *New York Times;* she had already performed internationally and is now a major international attraction. *United States* follows the general format of a concert. A series of songs is backed by slide and film projections and interspersed with monologues and physical images. Anderson created all of the material. She wrote the lyrics of the songs and composed the music. She wrote the stories and the dialogue. She created the projections and conceived the visual and aural effects. She is also the main performer—talking to the audience, creating physical or sound images, playing a violin or synthesizer, and singing. Except for the small combo that accompanies her and occasionally plays independently and for a few actors who appear briefly, *United States: Parts I–IV,* which lasts more than seven hours, is a one-woman performance.

The stories Anderson tells are all in the first person. Although they actually reveal little about her personality and private life, they help in relating her to a genre that could be called "autoperformance" that has developed recently in the avant-garde. The performance is usually a solo and is about, or derived directly from, the life of the performer. The performer performs herself and her life. This, in turn, is a subgenre of so-called "art performance" in which performance is equated with painting and sculpture, and performance "objects," usually created by artists who are not primarily theatre people, are exhibited in an art gallery context to an art world audience.

For years, Anderson did solo "art performances," presenting pieces in galleries, churches, loft theatres, and other alternative spaces. Sometimes she would talk, telling her "personal" stories, and play the violin. Sometimes she would create effects, using, for example, a violin that talked when a magnetic recording tape stretched in the violin bow was moved back and forth over the strings. Sometimes she used projections, such as the 8mm film of "her psychoanalyst" she projected on the small figure of a man. All of those art performance elements were combined in *United States*.

After parts I and II of *United States* had been completed but before the whole work had been shown, "Oh Superman," one of two songs from the early section that made up a small, privately printed record, appeared on the charts of "hit" songs in England, and Anderson was given a recording contract by Warner Brothers Records. Laurie Anderson's songs, in themselves, are not avant-garde. She is working in an established idiom: rock. Indeed, as she began to emphasize the rock music aspect of her performances, her dress and hair style took on punk characteristics. She began to dress in black, and her short hair became even shorter. Although the music itself has some structural resemblance in its dronelike, repeating, unmodulated, or slowly modulated chord progressions to that of avant-garde musicians such as Phil Glass and Steve Reich, it is still rock music—original and recognizable but within the genre. The songs may be taken out of the context of the performance to exist as artifacts in a larger popular culture. This is not unusual. It merely reverses the process by which popular records are commonly incorporated into avant-garde performances. Indeed, a prevalent contemporary way of making a performance is to string together a sequence of "borrowed" music, usually rock, and develop a visual image, using live performers and perhaps technology, for each piece of music. In both cases, the music itself is not avant-garde, but it is part of an avant-garde performance.

United States lacks any overall story. The entire performance, and each section of it, is given coherence by detailed formal connotations that do not explain each other or fit together intellectually to create larger groupings of information. The movement of a pointer swinging back and forth indicating the currents that supposedly carried Noah's ark from New York State to Ararat relates to the movement of Anderson's hand in front of her face as she talks about driving an automobile in the rain. These movements relate to the gesture for both "hello" and "goodbye" in the language of a gas station attendant who speaks in Anderson's own electronically altered voice. Later, Anderson raises her violin bow over her head and, swinging it back and forth, creates a screen that catches an image projected at an angle that makes it otherwise invisible to the audience. The image appears suddenly, hanging in the air over her head; the thin, moving "screen" echoes the earlier images.

Thus, in performance the songs become part of a larger whole that is the work of art. They are "tied in" primarily by repeated sensory and verbal imagery. Late in *United States*, for example, Anderson tells the story of how Thomas Edison went on a lecture tour to argue against the adoption of direct, rather than alternating, current. As a demonstration, he electrocuted a dog. There is no explanation for, or justification of, this unusual and gratuitous image. It does not seem to fit intellectually. But at a purely formal level, it does relate to other images scattered throughout *United States*. "Walkin' the Dog," for example—the flip side of the "Oh Superman" record—was sung earlier in the performance. Someone involved with the hermetic avant-garde can appreciate how structural connections work *against* meaning and distort it in Anderson's work. This formal structuring does not need to be understood for individual songs to be appreciated, but its effect is to help make *United States* more than a mere rock concert.

The avant-garde audience is interested, among other things, in the *way* in which art comments on society rather than in the content of that comment. To this audience, *United States* is a rock concert that comments on rock concerts. Just as Roy Lichtenstein's Pop Art paintings commented on comic strips by reproducing and enlarging details of the strips or Andy Warhol's silk-screened works and Campbell soup cans commented on the imagery of commercial mass production by copying that imagery, Anderson's long piece refers to a rock concert by being not exactly a rock concert. The stories and imagery, not found in a rock concert, are as important as the songs. Unlike most rock singers—and unlike the antagonistic avant-garde—her manner and attitude are not at all aggressive or abrasive. She does not "sell" the material. She is relaxed, informal, precise, clear, and pleasant—a great contrast to most rock singers. Rock concerts are not presented at the Brooklyn Academy of Music. *United States* can be seen as a rock concert by and for the avant-garde. As Laurie Anderson's work demonstrates, the avant-garde did not die; it shifted from its antagonistic to its hermetic form.

Within the subculture of the avant-garde, there are at least two possibilities for theatre—an audience composed of those interested primarily in arts other than drama, and an audience oriented exclusively toward theatre. Either could be potentially antagonistic or hermetic. We could have an antagonistic avant-garde based in several of the arts or a hermetic avant-garde concentrating on drama. Historically, however, a strong element of the 1960s antagonistic avant-garde was oriented toward drama. The current hermetic avant-garde theatre is oriented primarily, sometimes exclusively, toward the other arts.

Jerzy Grotowski's idea of a "Poor Theatre," which was so influential in the 1960s, consciously excluded the other arts in order to "purify" theatre—to make it do what only theatre, and not the other arts, could do. In itself, Grotowski's Polish Laboratory Theatre was hermetic. It did not attempt to reach a large or general public, and it severely limited the number of its performances and the size of its audiences. It did not attempt to change society or to confront the bourgeoisie. It involved an intense, psychologically isolating, quasi-religious belief in theatre and the "holy actor."

Grotowski's actor-training techniques, his neo-Expressionist acting style, and his altering of the traditional audience-performance relationship had strong influence, however, on the antagonistic avant-garde of the 1960s. With the addition of antiestablishment content, his ideas were modified and developed to confront and confound the bourgeoisie—at least in our final conspiratorial model of that form that includes a sympathetic rather than a bourgeois audience.

The current hermetic avant-garde art world, as represented by Laurie Anderson, contains few theatre people—most have little interest in other art forms—and is influenced primarily by arts other than drama. Anderson studied the violin when she was young, her college education was in the visual arts, and she has exhibited in art galleries. Her performances make use of and relate to music and the visual arts and appeal to those audiences. They have little or no relationship to drama (or to dance). Much of the antagonistic avant-garde of the 1960s—as represented by, for example, the Living Theatre—was concerned primarily with drama. Judith Malina and Julian Beck, the founders of the Living Theatre, were trained theatre people; their theatre was drama-oriented.

There is little or no acting in a Laurie Anderson performance. In *United States*, performers other than Anderson appear only briefly to act dialogue. Sometimes, in the course of telling a story, Anderson "acts" the voice of herself and/or other characters, perhaps with the help of electronic alteration. Usually, she may be said to act only in the sense that her material, which seems spontaneous, has been memorized.

This does not mean that all of today's avant-garde rejects acting. John Jesurun, for example, is a visual artist—among other things, he created installations using stuffed birds—who became a filmmaker and then began to stage his own plays. Working in the Pyramid Club—a small, punk, store-front discotheque on the Lower East Side of Manhattan— Jesurun put on a new half-hour installment of *Chang in a Void Moon* every Monday for forty-four weeks in 1982–83. He uses actors—many of them experienced Off-Off-Broadway actors—but the performance style relates to, and derives from, film rather than the stage. It does not depend on actor-training methods to develop stamina, flexibility, projection, and so forth; in contrast to much of the 1960s work, it makes little physical demand on the performer. In this work, even the acting relates most strongly to an art other than drama.

A second basic difference between the present avant-garde and that of the 1960s is that current work tends to be formal and conceptual rather than content-oriented. The continuously evolving stories of *Chang in a Void Moon* have no more message than an old "B" movie or film serial; they are merely a framework upon which visual and verbal "ideas" develop. Although one might expect a comprehensive and pointed sociopolitical statement from a piece titled *United States: Parts I–IV*, this was not the case. Meanings and messages, often ironic or satirical, can be found in Anderson's work, but they do not create a coherent whole, and literal intellectual content is not their most important aspect.

The profound division in avant-garde performance between drama and the other arts can be both illustrated and explained by the way the different disciplines are taught in our colleges and universities. The history of the visual arts since the late nineteenth century is presented primarily as consisting of the avant-garde; without the avant-garde, there would be no history of painting and sculpture. The history of theatre, on the other hand, usually ignores the avant-garde completely or relegates it to a very minor position. A history of the theatre that refers to playwriting and the classics is possible without reference to the avant-garde. Yet, at least in its sociocultural origins, the avant-garde is the same in all the arts.

Whereas the emphasis in the visual arts is on aesthetics, theatre is taught as a commercial and popular enterprise relating to box office success. The visual arts are dealt with formally; theatre is taught as consisting of message, content, and sociopolitical import. Thus the teaching of theatre is primarily mainstream and traditional, oriented toward Broadway, "Great Plays" (still Tennessee Williams and Arthur Miller), the genres of tragedy and comedy, Shakespeare and the classics. Beckett is presented as representing the contemporary avant-garde. It is a literary approach.

The teaching of dance seems to be an exception to this general dichotomy, however. College dance departments, in general, tend to support the new as well as the traditional. Some even teach postmodern dance. Many avant-garde dancers tour the colleges. Although much of the writing about dance is impressionistic, it often possesses a strong for-mal slant, perhaps because dance is relatively removed from the dynam-ics of the society. It may be for this reason that avant-garde dance is much more energized and active in New York than is avant-garde drama.

Each year, visual arts departments and, to a lesser extent, dance de-partments graduate many people with an established and defined inter-est in the avant-garde, people who are able to appreciate formal and conceptual values. The same is not true of theatre departments. Thus the young audiences for current performances tend to come from disciplines other than theatre. Whereas the antagonistic avant-garde of the 1960s related to the traditions of dramatic literature by staging radical versions of Shakespeare and the classics, contemporary avant-garde performance offers little to those who are drama-oriented.

Because critics are to a great extent the products of our educational system, the criticism of theatre differs from that of the visual arts. Art criti-cism is concerned with formal analysis and a discussion of the way art comments on art in a historical dialogue. Theatre criticism deals primarily with psychosociopolitical interpretations and value judgments. None of the three reviews of *United States* in the same issue of the *Village Voice*—Anderson is, after all, a major figure—discussed the formal as-pects of the piece. All searched for "big" meanings and, finding none, were disparaging and uninterested. Such critical response merely indi-cates the psychological polarity that exists in both avant-garde perfor-mance and the larger society.

Thus by referring to an unusual performance that took place many years ago, we have been led to the examination of a dichotomy in avant-garde theatre. On one hand, we have performances oriented to-ward drama, expressive acting, meaning, and content. On the other hand, we have performances oriented toward other arts—painting, sculpture, music, film, poetry—and toward formalism. This is not a bad situation or a good one. Not everyone should have the same taste. But the analysis does give us a way of explaining both recent developments in avant-garde theatre and the dynamics of the avant-garde within to-day's society.

structuralist theatre

Historically, formalism in theatre has been more or less synonymous with style, with abstraction. It has been a theatre of visual and auditory formalism that related to painting and music and emphasized the senses. Vsevolod Meyerhold, for example, was famous for his formalist, stylized interpretations of realistic scripts (indeed, the "crime" with which Meyerhold was charged, and for which he died, was "formalism"). Almost always, formalism in theatre has been subservient to content. The people who emphasized formal elements felt that these elements most clearly supported and helped to express the intellectual material, message, or theme. Historically, a formalist production used form to make its meaning or the feelings attached to that meaning more significant, clearer, and more powerful.

Even today, formalist theatre uses form as style, as abstraction, even though meaning is no longer of primary importance. It is a visual theatre, a painterly theatre, a retinal theatre, a "theatre of images."

In this part of the book, a new kind of formalism is discussed. Here, the forms employed are mental rather than sensory. They tend to be intellectual and even logical rather than intuitive and impressionistic. They work against meaning and representational feeling rather than suggesting and supporting it.

This new formalism can be called Structuralist theatre. Structuralist theatre works with structure in a formal way and makes structure—the relationship between the parts—the most important aesthetic element in the performance. (An analysis of performance structure was made in Chapter 2.) Since the relationship between the parts exists to a great extent in time, and since it involves connections between moments or sections of the play through or over or across time, this kind of formalism tends to involve time more than the present moment, the mind more than the eye and the ear.

The structure of a performance is completely independent of visual style. The same structures may underlie any style. The way the performers work, the design of costumes and decor, the atmosphere of the presentation, and so on, have no necessary relationship to the structure. Thus any visual style may be used in staging a Structuralist play. This is most apparent in the realistic Structuralist plays that are described in the following chapters, such as *Revolutionary Dance, The Marilyn Project,* and *Double Gothic.* In these performances, the visual style is not formal; the experience is. Other of the Structuralist productions described here are not realistic, however. One, *Iowa Transfer,* uses almost no acting and could not even be called a play.

In this part, we see examples of how theatrical theory—the analysis of structure—can be consciously and intentionally used to make a performance. The performances began not with a feeling or idea about life that needed to be expressed but with an idea about theatrical structure. That was the most important thing. At least in my own work, theory and practice have constantly fed and enriched each other.

the structuralist workshop

The Structuralist Workshop, a theatre group of which I am the artistic director, attempts to use structural analysis as an approach to performance. The workshop is involved with what it calls "Structuralism" in theatre. Some have claimed that this use of the word is improper. "The term 'structuralism,'" they say, "already refers to certain philosophies, to certain kinds of thought. Indeed, the intellectual popularity of structural linguistics and structural anthropology might almost be described as a fad. 'Structuralism' can't be used now to apply to something else." This, of course, is not persuasive. Many words have multiple meanings. The important thing is to understand, through its context, how the word is being used in each instance. It is even possible to capitalize "Structuralism" (like Futurism and Surrealism) when it refers to a particular artistic movement and to leave it uncapitalized when it refers to a general philosophy. A word such as "structuralism" is not a registered trademark. Words are often taken from one discipline for use in another. (Why theatre is almost always behind philosophy, science, and the other arts is a different question.) After all, the word "Structuralism" is extremely precise and accurate. What else would you call aesthetic theory that emphasizes and gives primary importance to structure?

At one level there is a pronounced similarity between the analytical structuralism of structural linguistics, structural anthropology, and the like and the theories of theatrical Structuralism. As their names indicate, they have a common belief in the importance of structure. Yet their views of structure are quite different.

Neither structural linguistics nor structural anthropology studies experience as such. A phenomenon—a sentence, a myth—is not analyzed for its *own* unique structure. It is compared to other sentences, other myths, to enable one to understand structures that lie behind or beyond experience. The intent is to make clear unconscious patterns and structures. In *Structural Anthropology*, Claude Lévi-Strauss explains:

If, as we believe to be the case, the unconscious activity of the mind consists in imposing forms upon content, and if these forms are fundamentally the same for all minds—ancient and modern, primitive and civilized (as the study of the symbolic function, expressed in language, so strikingly indicates)—it is necessary and sufficient to grasp the unconscious structure underlying each institution and each custom, in order to obtain a principle of interpretation valid for other institutions and other customs, provided of course that the analysis is carried far enough.

It is difficult to see why analytical systems that attempt to clarify unconscious structures would be used as theatrical theory to create performances. According to the systems themselves, *every* performance is naturally a product of unconscious material. In some cases analysis might be difficult, but one performance would not have more or less structure than another.

(In his search for "natural bases" of the phonemic system—for a basic structure in the brain—Lévi-Strauss accepts evidence that seems to show similar patterns of synesthesia—in this case, color/vowel correspondences—among people with the same mother tongue. Unfortunately, this theory is not correct. Even synesthetic members of the same family may demonstrate different systems of correspondence. Yet until some evidence is found for a natural base for phonemic structure, the possibility will exist that so-called "unconscious structures" are being imposed by the analyst rather than discovered. At any rate, theatrical Structuralism is not concerned with the structure of the brain but with the workings of the mind and the unique structure of particular experiences.)

If a system of structural analysis is thought to apply to all theatre, any presentation could be a manifestation of it. How, then, can analysis be turned into usable theory for the creation of performance? A particular "angle," a special "slant," a certain prejudice, is needed. For the Structuralist Workshop this is found in the effort to make structure of prime importance. All theatre has structure, but seldom is it the primary aspect. Although they use many styles and various kinds of performing, all of the productions of the workshop demonstrate this attempt to make structure dominate.

The most difficult problems in doing so relate to meaning. If a performance has no meaning—as in music and dance—it is relatively easy to make structure predominate. In drama, however, structure has long been used to support and clarify meaning. Therefore, where meaning exists, it tends to take over. The spectator assumes that, since there are semantic elements, the presentation should be understood semantically. Material is interpreted; meanings are "read in" where they were not intended.

One critic, describing my *Revolutionary Dance*, wrote: "A story-line begins to evolve . . . and incorporates into its narrative." There was no story or narrative. I had written seven short scenes about people who were not in the military—they did not wear uniforms—engaged in some sort of civil war in an unnamed country. Each of them used some, but not necessarily all, of certain basic movements and speeches that I wanted to make into structural repetitions. The scenes were put together in a certain order after they were written. They could have gone in any order. It was the repetitions that mattered. One incident did not cause another. Ten actors each played several different characters; no characters appeared in more than one scene. In one scene, two actors might be on the same side in the war; in a later scene, they might be on opposite sides. An actor playing a man who was obviously dead in one scene appeared alive in a later scene. The cast was international: two Italians, three Iranians, a Korean, a Filipino, an Israeli, and two Americans. The costumes and props were contemporary; the unstated time was the present (or future). Yet the same critic explained that the play was "apparently an off-shoot of the Bicentennial spirit" and spoke of "patriotic fervor."

Of course, there is no defense against such interpretations. If people commonly see meaningful figures in the inkblots of the Rorschach test, they may see meaning in any performance. If an observer sees a narrative where none was intended, that structure exists. Yet for the Structuralist trying to design particular experiences, the tendency for meaning to become ascendant is a problem that must be considered.

To examine the relationship between structure and meaning, to see how an attempt may be made to make structure dominant, and as practical examples of the application of Structuralist theory, let us look at some of the presentations of the Structuralist Workshop.

In the opening scene of Bill Simmer's *Satellite Salad*, a woman sits alone, knitting in a rocking chair. She looks up as if someone were there and speaks: "I'm older than I look." There is a pause, and she speaks again. "No, on the contrary, I'm flattered." "A little bumpy," she says. The scene continues in this way, with only the woman speaking. One probably realizes that only one-half of a conversation is being presented. Perhaps this creates the expectancy that, later in the play, the unheard portion of the dialogue will be revealed. If so, it will probably be extremely meaningful. There may be a tendency to listen more carefully than usual to the woman's words so that the "blanks" may be filled in and/or the phrases recognized if they are repeated later. During the second scene of the play, which involves two actors, and the third scene, which involves three actors, there are also sections in which the performers speak to an invisible and silent character. This probably intensifies the expectancy—or creates it, if it does not already exist—that the secret of the unheard speeches will be revealed later in the play.

Information structures, thematic structures, and structural repetition coexist in *Satellite Salad*. The stories of the characters in the one-person, two-person, and three-person scenes seem to relate and weave together. Images of salad and satellite recur, verbally and visually. Material from the three basic stories appears again and again in a fourth situation: three actors improvising for an acting teacher.

At the end of Simmer's play, the incomplete scenes of the opening are indeed completed.

> AGENT: I must say, I'm a little surprised, meeting you. I expected a much older woman.
> MADELINE: I'm older than I look.
> AGENT: Of course. (Pause) I hope you don't mind my saying that.
> MADELINE: No, on the contrary, I'm flattered.
> AGENT: I'm glad. We're going to hit it off just fine, I can tell already. (Pause) Did you have a good flight?
> MADELINE: A little bumpy.

Expectancies have been fulfilled, bridging the complex, full-length work. They provide a sense of resolution, of ending. They do not explain anything, however. The three "invisible" characters now made tangible are not the people they are thought to be by the others in the scene: each of the three actors is improvising in the given situation of a "final assignment." The informational connections between the four sets of characters have been for the sake of structure itself rather than to create an overall meaning. The process of addition can be interesting or significant, even if no overall total is obtained.

Nor does the thematic structure of the work relate to the informational structure in any consistent way. Simmer explains that his creation of the piece began when a friend said she wanted to sing the song "Satellite of Love" in the planned production. He used those images, but they probably could have been any others.

Robb Creese works with visual and aural patterns. They are determined very early in the creative process and are basically independent of the semantic, acted material. Creese's *Discrete Scenepoints* used three different performing areas (see figure). In each, a geometrical figure was marked on the floor with tape. The first figure was a triangle. It was surrounded by three tables containing, respectively, flowers, cups, and

books and candles. The second area, somewhat larger, contained a pentagon or five-sided figure surrounded by low furniture: a bed, a chair, a
low table, and other pieces. The vertices of the pentagon were connected by tape lines. In the third area was a still larger seven-sided figure,
its vertices also connected by lines. There was no furniture around it. The
play was performed in each of these areas in sequence. In each of the
thirteen sections, action began in the triangle, switched to the pentagon,
and then took place on the heptagon. A spatial sequence of scenes was
followed throughout the play.

In each area, movement was primarily along the lines of the figures;
performers were stationary only at vertices (or used the furniture at the
vertices of the pentagon). In each of the thirteen sections, movement
possibilities were limited in the same way in each of the three areas. The
first unit was titled "One Point to the Right"; only the first and second
vertices of each figure were used. By unit six, "Six Points to the Right," all
of the vertices of the heptagon were in use and pieces of furniture at the
vertices of the pentagon were being used more than once. When the
pattern developed into skipping points—unit ten, for example, was "Skip
Two Points to the Right"—performers began to move along the diagonals
of the heptagon. Thus the blocking of the scenes was obviously patterned.

The type of performance was different in each of the three areas. In
the first, only single actors spoke (in part, about medieval symbolism of
flowers, cups, books and candles), although at times the requirements of
the blocking patterns turned them away from some, or all, of the spectators. In the second, actors played ostensibly realistic scenes. In the third,
they declaimed portions of medieval cycle plays. The second unit used
images, phrases, names, ideas, and elements from both the preceding
solo in the triangle area and the following scene in the heptagon.

Speech in the third (medieval cycle play) section of each unit followed
strict patterns that ignored punctuation and the distinction between
characters. In the first unit, for example, Creese created new "lines," each
composed of two seven-word phrases. The first phrase was emphasized
/xxXxxXX/, and the second phrase was emphasized /xXxXXXx/—all ac-
cented words and all unaccented words being delivered with more or
less equal volume. Thus, the script reads, in part:

ANTHONY [*the names of the actors were used rather than those of the characters*]: . . . WORTH more am I THAN—he WILL be AND TO PROVE it / i will
SIT in god's SEAT ON—high WITH sun AND MOON AND stars / on sky I am
now SET AS—you MAY see NOW PRAISE ME here / in this SEAT . . .
ROBBEE: god we MIGHT CURSE—and TAKE thee AS FAR MORE worth / we
fall DOWN at thy SEAT . . .

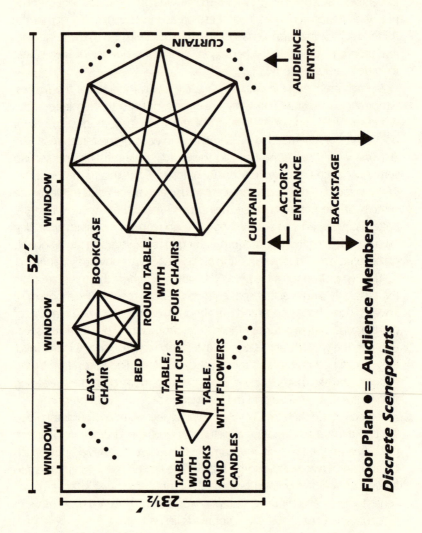

Floor Plan ● = Audience Members
Discrete Scenepoints

A pattern—the regular repetition of elements—has the potential of heightening the certainty of expectations. When patterned wallpaper disappears around a corner, we are quite certain how the wall will look, even though we have not yet seen it. This does not mean, however, that all patterns are equally predictable or even equally recognizable. Robb Creese's *Star 17 + 70 + 6* used, among other patterns, units composed of seventeen lines of seventeen syllables. Few, if any, spectators could be expected to discern such a pattern. Yet, even though the listener is not conscious of a particular pattern and cannot say what it is, it could be assumed to have an effect—as would unrecognized musical patterns. Creese uses patterns at basic levels of a performance to present structure, as he says, "without regard to subject matter or theme."

My own play, *Eight People,* made extensive use of nonsemantic repetition. It presented eight people/characters in twenty-five short scenes that suggested an inconclusive story of love and espionage—probably industrial espionage. Narrative was intentionally repressed so that structural elements would be relatively more important.

Let us look at brief selected moments in several of the early scenes. In the first scene, a young woman with a suitcase is sitting in a church. A man speaks to her quietly in Italian, "E questa la valigia?" She answers, "Of course."

In the second scene, a telephone conversation, a man questions a woman to be sure that the motor she has developed really runs properly: "Are you sure it works?"

In the third scene, a young woman in a nightgown is writing by candlelight. A young man enters, saying he cannot sleep. "You could turn on the lights, you know. You don't have to write in the dark. Sometimes I think I don't know very much about you."

In the fourth scene, three men are drinking. Two are Italians we have seen in the church. The woman who was with them is dancing. One of the men stops her. There is a discussion. "I drink to Ela, who is angry," says the man, raising his glass. "Salute!" "It's nothing to worry about," the woman says. "It doesn't matter."

In the fifth scene, the man who could not sleep is talking in a business office to the woman who spoke on the telephone: "You're not Polish, are you? I've got a Polish joke." "It's all right," she answers, "you can tell me." A moment later, he asks if he can use her telephone. "Sure, why not?" she says. "Is anything the matter?"

In the seventh scene, the man who spoke Italian in the church and was one of the men in the drinking scene is talking on a park bench to the woman who was writing at night. He says that he is speaking for the other Italian man: "You know Mario is very shy." "No, I didn't know that." "It's a rather difficult situation. He wants to talk to you himself, but he can't. He's very shy."

In the ninth scene, all of these moments are referred to in one brief exchange. The inventor has met a Mr. Kim, whom she mentioned in the telephone call. As they start to leave, she stops.

> EDNA: Do you live in the North, near the mountains?
> WOO OK: No, of course not. Is anything the matter?
> EDNA: It's a rather difficult situation. I just wanted to be sure. I don't know very much about you.
> WOO OK: That's all right. It doesn't matter.

They exit. In this short passage of dialogue, the spectator may hear many echoes and half-echoes from earlier scenes. He might even remember that, in the drinking scene, one of the men had said, "I live in the North, near the mountains."

Repetitions occur naturally in real life, and the repetition of an ordinary phrase like "Of course not" and "That's all right" might not enter the spectator's conscious awareness. But other, more unusual phrases such as "It's a rather difficult situation" tend to call attention to themselves and to be noticed consciously.

In addition to phrases of dialogue, many other elements were repeated for nonsyntactic structural reasons in *Eight People*. Gestures recurred: in several scenes, a person held out a rake at arm's length, its handle vertical and the teeth pointed toward the ground. In most of the twenty-five scenes, paper was torn in one way or another. After the Italian man asked the woman about the suitcase in the church, she gave him a letter, which he opened, read, and ripped up; the man talking on the telephone to the inventor tore open a package of cookies and ate them; when the young man interrupted the woman's writing at night, she ripped up her manuscript. Even the spatial and movement patterns of actors were repeated; in each of three different scenes, one of the three women stood in the center of a triangle formed by three other people and turned to face each one as they spoke.

The same or similar objects appeared and reappeared: umbrellas, rakes, tape recorders, suitcases. Every third scene was a telephone call. Sounds recurred: the telephone was heard ringing again and again; in the quiet and intimate production, the soft sound of leaves being raked or walked through was heard over and over.

As the examples have shown, the various repetitions in *Eight People* functioned in part at a semantic level. Each was justified by the realistic context of the scene and contributed to the accumulating information about character, situation, action, and so on. If each was taken only in its momentary context—if its quality as repetition was removed—there would be nothing unrealistic about it. Unlike the repeated phrase that helps to create and emphasize the character of a single person, however, the repetitions of *Eight People* occurred between characters rather than consistently within a character. This tended to make their nonsemantic attributes dominate. Their pure alogical aspects were "pulled out" "in front of" their realistic logical context.

If structure in performance is conceived of as a dynamic concept, the examples from *Eight People* can be seen to be dynamic to different degrees. (Of course, this should not be taken as a value judgment. Structure is not better or worse because it is more or less dynamic. Strong and weak structures vary in quality; their worth is a question of personal taste.) For example, until near the end, every third scene in *Eight People* involved a telephone conversation that began with the sound of a phone being dialed and a phone ringing. This is not a repetition that easily captures conscious attention. Perhaps because the ringing of a phone is so common in everyday life, its ringing several times in a performance does not lead us to expect it to ring again, nor, when it does ring, does it tend to remind us of the previous times. It can be accepted as purely functional. Nor was there any tension between the phone ringing and its context. It did not tend to be "false" because it had—like a phrase spoken previously by a different character—been heard before in a different syntactical web. Of course, as one of many repetitions in *Eight People*, the ringing phones did attract formal attention, but the nonsemantic qualities of the repetition did not force themselves as strongly on the attention as did others. The nonsemantic aspects of the ripping of paper, on the other hand, were easily established. Spectators soon began to anticipate that more paper would be torn. When paper appeared, they may have waited for it to be ripped up—something that did not always happen. After one performance, a spectator ostentatiously ripped up the program. The performance element was highly dynamic structurally.

One indication of the dynamic aspects of nonsemantic structure was found in anecdotal reports by spectators of *Eight People*. Frequently they explained that they had continued to think about the performance, that they had dreamed about it, that they had been more involved with it in retrospect than they had when it was being presented. It was as if the mind, once started on the anticipation of and search for structural repetition, did not stop the way of functioning "programmed" by the performance. In the play, small details—the sound of paper being torn, a particular phrase, a gesture—were pulled out of their context by their structural importance; they were made to seem large in comparison to their realistic "size" and importance. Thus one spectator attributed to the play the great impact on him, soon after the performance, of a small incident—a door opening in a long corridor. There were no doors in the production, which was done in the round, but since nonsemantic structure deals with the pure workings of the mind, it is the way the mind functions, rather than the informational context, that is significant.

chapter 9

three structuralist performances

The first of the three productions described in this chapter, my *Iowa Transfer*, does not use acting—at least not very much of it. It is more closely related to a Happening than to a play. (I worked in Happenings for several years, and my Structuralist plays developed out of them. My first Structuralist play—any work that uses acting extensively may be called a play because the performers "play" at being someone else— was *Room 706*, done in 1966. The chronology of this development from Happenings to Structuralism has been documented in my book *The Art of Time*.) In *Iowa Transfer*, structural repetition of a limited number of discrete images is juxtaposed with the recreation of a nonnarrative incident that extends through time.

The Marilyn Project was not written with Structuralism in mind, and the script by David Gaard is not at all Structuralist. The director, Richard Schechner, imposed an original, precise, and complex physical structure on the piece when he staged it at the Performing Garage in 1975.

The third production, my *Double Gothic*, also demonstrates how spatial structure can be a dominant aspect of the presentation. Here, through a special "perceptual machine," the spatial structure is not immediately apparent but is revealed and develops through time. Any play could have been done in the construction. Granted, the blackness was more fitting—in a traditional semiotic sense—for a serious play such as a Gothic than it would have been for a comedy, but most of my other plays could have been done there quite well. The physical presentation was a more or less independent variable not intended to express a central theme or convey part of a unified message. It derived from concerns with organizing experience rather than concerns with conveying information.

Iowa Transfer

I had never been to Iowa City and did not know the space where the performance would be staged, but that did not affect the concept of the piece. I wanted to transfer exterior spaces—various spaces around the theatre in the university and the city—not merely into the theatre itself but into the minds of the spectators. If, the theory went, viewers saw pictures of a particular action being done in a specific locale outside of the theatre, they would, when presented with the same action in the theatre, tend to see the remembered landscape "around" or "clinging to" the activity. The performance would be an attempt to stimulate, through memory, active projective (nonintellectual) thought in the spectator.

As in my sculpture, the pictures—in this case slide projections—would be taken simultaneously. Three camerapeople would photograph an action at the same instant; they would move and shoot again; then move for a third set of simultaneous pictures. The three photographs taken at the same time would be projected simultaneously side by side during the performance. Each set of nine slides would show the development of the target action in time and the movement (or occasional nonmovement) of the camerapeople. It would not give a single subjective view and/or interpretation of the activity but would tend toward objectivity, the three views creating a "parapersonal" picture of the action. (Indeed, the shooting sequences were not planned; each cameraperson moved as he or she wished, and the simultaneous shooting was coordinated by a crew chief.)

I wanted a rowboat in the performance. Primarily, it was to establish a clear physical barrier (the water) between the camerapeople and the action. Small actions done in and around the boat would be invisible or indistinct to cameras on the banks, but, by placing one of the cameras in the boat where it could record the action clearly, the disparity between the three viewpoints' pictures could be emphasized. After I had decided to use a boat, a friend who had attended the university told me that a river did, indeed, flow through the campus.

I also decided to do something with or about dogs in the performance. They would not be central to the piece—they would not be photographed by teams of camerapeople—but, like the actions we would perform, I saw them as scattered throughout the countryside. The spectator might be made aware of both dogs and places outside the theatre; like the spaces, images of dogs might also be "transferred."

Like my other works, the piece would be structural. The main emphasis would be on the connections between the parts—on the structural relationships. Several activities would be repeated over and over, each repetition relating to the others of the same kind. Each action, repeated in both sets of slides and by "live" performers, would create a "web" or irregular pattern of interrelationships. The piece would be composed of several "webs" overlapping each other and the continuous core action of the boat.

When spectators enter the South Hall of the Old Music Building at 8:30 on Sunday, November 23, 1975, they face an arc of three low wooden risers holding folding chairs. High at the rear center of the arc is a long table with three slide projectors on it. The room is large and the seating section stops well short of the walls; there is space around and behind the spectators. On the wooden floor in front of them—at the focus-point of the crescent of chairs—is a large, empty, metal rowboat.

In the gathering audience are two large dogs. Their masters have taken them to opposite ends of the seating crescent. As spectators find seats, one of the dogs barks occasionally. Soon, although people tend to keep some distance from the dogs, the audience section is almost filled. Some people sit on the floor.

The "overture" to the performance is a tape recording:

FIRST MAN: It's alright
We were interested in askin' you if—a—
There's gonna be a multimedia presentation on Sunday evening at 8:30—a—in the Old Music Building. . . .
SECOND MAN: Yeah.
FM: And we're looking for people that h . . . own dogs and want to find out if they . . . you'd be willing to come to the Old Music Building at 8:30 on Sunday evening for this performance that's going to take place there. It's a multimedia performance
SM: I don't understand. Down boy!
FM: Just this crazy kind of thing is going to go on. What it involves is us going out and recording people that ha . . . own dogs, and while I'm recording our conversation, he's taking pictures of it. And during the performance there will be a slide projector showing these photographs of you and your dog. If you're there at the same time that the slides are being shown, it's like the real thing and then the image of the real thing happening at the same time. And so—that's pretty much what it is. But it doesn't matter, if you want to come or not.
SM: Like where's this at now?
FM: This is at the Old Music Building. You know where East Hall is?
SM: Uhg ugh.
FM: Are you a student?
SM: No.
FM: Oh, OK.
SM: Do you have to be a student?
FM: No. But if you were a student, then you'd know more.

SM: No, like . . . I don't know. Probably. It sounds fairly interesting.
FM: 8:30 Sunday night.
SM: It's called . . . a? What's it called again?
FM: Old Music Building, the South—
SM: No. What's this thing called?
FM: This'll be . . . a . . . *Iowa Transference.*

On the tape that is opening *Iowa Transfer,* other attempts to get dogs to attend the performance are heard. "What kind of a dog is it?" "What are they going to do with all these dogs?"

Then, although the spectator does not now realize what they are, tape recordings made during the photographing of the actions are played. Crew people can be heard discussing their assignments. "OK, let's do this in front of the Physics Building." "Wait for the bus!" ". . . one camera 150 feet up in one building." Frequently the crew chief can be heard counting to cue the camerapeople. "Cameras ready! One. Two. Three."

There are also taped passages of interviews with bystanders. "I think it lacks aesthetic integrity." "So he has something in mind." "There doesn't seem to be a great deal of purpose in their actions." Of course, background noises can be heard, too—particularly in a large dining hall or restaurant—and perhaps these sounds will be related by the spectator to images in the later sets of slides.

Now only dim lights are on in the large space. The main part of *Iowa Transfer* begins. In front of the audience, near the blank wall that the spectators face, people pour three buckets of colored water one at a time down an inclined plastic sheet. Briefly, the transparent plastic is (let's say) yellow, then blue, then red.

The three slide projectors come on, and three slides are projected on the blank wall. They show the metal rowboat with two people in it on a lake. (The river had proved too dangerous.) All three pictures have been taken at the same moment from different angles and distances. One camera is on shore, one on a wooden pier, and one on a floating dock.

They approximate the vertices of a triangle with the boat in the center. (If one looks carefully, photographers taking simultaneous pictures can sometimes be seen in a slide.) Another set of black-and-white slides, and then a third set, show the movement of the boat into the space between the cameras.

Two people in winter coats and clothing have climbed into the metal rowboat that sits in front of the spectators. One of them moves the oars as the other switches on a large tape recorder in the boat. The loud amplified sound is of water, oars, people moving about and talking. (This tape, made in the rowboat during shooting, remained unedited. It lasted about thirty-five minutes and played throughout the performance.) The people in the boat keep their movements more or less related to the tape; sometimes they speak the same words at the same time—it is their own voices that are heard on the tape.

Now three people are moving out into the performance space with large white panels. They place the panels next to each other to form a wall. Then the white wall dissolves, and the panels go off in various directions.

As the actions are performed, the tape recording continues to play loudly from the boat. Three people—one at the audience right, one at the left, and one behind the projector table behind the audience—throw white ropes to the boat and pretend to take photographs of it. (The throwing of each rope was an action recorded by the photographers at the lake.) They synchronize their movements with the sounds on the tape. Sometimes when their voices are heard on the tape, they call out the same words, "Cameras ready. One. Two." Questions and directions are called among the camerapeople; the people in the boat converse with the people on land.

Slides go on, another simultaneous set of three. The performers become motionless. They might be frozen in the middle of an action. Perhaps the slides show three people carrying eight-foot wooden poles through a crowded campus restaurant. As the slide sequence progresses, the people bring the poles together to form a triangle.

The slides go off. The action related to the tape recording continues. "Am I supposed to keep this rope?" "Barbara does a drawing." "You can rest the oars."

Performers are again moving in the space around the boat and at the sides of the spectators. Perhaps a person places a chair in a corner of the room and sits in it; others tape a plastic sheet to the walls and floor in front of the chair, making a transparent plastic wall that seals the person in. The person rises, breaks the plastic, steps through it, and moves away.

Slides come on; the action stops. Perhaps the pictures show three large white panels being assembled into a wall across railroad tracks on a bridge. Perhaps they show three eight-foot wooden poles being leaned parallel to each other and about three feet apart against a rusted water tank.

When the sequence of slides—three sets of three—is over, the action in the boat and in the performance space recommences. At one point, one of the camerapeople who have been photographing the boat climbs aboard the boat. Then small constructions are built in the boat; drawings are made and thrown overboard. From the tape, the spectator might deduce that these activities, too, are being (had been) photographed.

Several teams of live performers are working in the space. (They do not have fixed times or places to perform; their activity is ordered and controlled by their crew chiefs.) The materials they use for their activities—the poles, panels, and so forth—are stored near the walls at each side of the audience. They move out in the performance space—perhaps two or more groups are working at once—perform their actions and return the materials.

There are only a few actions. Each is repeated many times in different places, perhaps by different people. The wall is built of white panels. The three poles are formed into a triangle. Poles are leaned against a wall parallel to each other. A person sitting in a chair is sealed into a corner with transparent plastic and leaves, breaking the plastic. Two people create a transparent wall by stretching out a large sheet of plastic fastened between the wooden poles they hold; a second wall is built, parallel to the first; and then a third. (This action requires six performers.)

These same actions, as well as those involving the boat—the throwing of ropes, the making of drawings, and so forth—are seen in the sequences of slides that interrupt the live action. A sitting woman is sealed behind plastic in the corner of a roadhouse; she breaks out, leaving the empty chair and ripped plastic. The three transparent walls are built momentarily in the middle of a moderately busy street; cars and pedestrians can be seen through the layers of plastic and around them. (The activities in and with the boat are not shown in chronological order in the slides; those sequences are projected randomly interspersed with the sequences of the other actions.)

Now the boat is returning to land, its activities ended. The tape stops. The performers are quiet and motionless. Again the plastic sheet is stretched at an incline in front of the spectators as it was at the beginning of the performance. Again a performer tilts a bucket over it, pouring. But the bucket is empty. There is no colored water. A second empty bucket is poured, and a third. The performers go off. *Iowa Transfer* is over.

The Marilyn Project

The Marilyn Project, a new play by David Gaard, was being presented in a special performance for the Directors' Unit of the Actors' Studio. Richard Schechner, who had directed *The Marilyn Project,* was moving about watching the actors from various vantage points. He stopped to talk quietly and briefly with one of the spectators. "This," he said as he moved away, "is my contribution to the Structuralist movement."

In what sense could Gaard's script and Schechner's staging of it be called "structuralist"? Of course, the answer will depend on how the term is defined. If structuralism in theatre means that particular emphasis has been given to the structure of the presentation or that something unusual has been done with the structure, *The Marilyn Project* fits the definition.

When the spectators climbed a long flight of stairs at the Performing Garage and entered the large rectangular room, they saw a single row of seats along three of the walls. Above these seats were narrow wooden platforms from which spectators also could look down at the performance. Two low risers with furniture on them had been placed near the long fourth wall of the room; members of the audience were allowed to stand behind them along the wall. Thus the playing space occupied the center of the rectangular room, and spectators were spaced side by side around the perimeter. Most of the spectators watched from three sides, however, and the risers tended to establish an "upstage" or rear area on the fourth side. The standing spectators were "behind" the risers, "offstage," and the opposite long side of the playing area became the "front." (The platforms, seats, risers, and so forth were referred to in the program as an "environment.")

On each of the two identical risers were an adjustable barber's chair and a makeup table. Above each chair and angled toward it hung two large mirrors. Two padded rubbing tables stood side by side in the space between the risers. In the main playing area there were two large floodlights on wheeled stands that raised them above head-height, four director's chairs, and two television cameras on stands. At an early point, the spectators realized that one end of the rectangular acting area was exactly like the other. It was as if a giant mirror had been placed across the short axis of the room: half of the room "reflected" the other half.

When the performance began, the double "reflection" was obvious. Two casts of actors, one at each end of the space, performed the play simultaneously. They were dressed alike. They spoke the same words at the same time. Their movements were the same, except that they mirrored each other: corresponding figures would move toward or away from the imaginary central mirror at the same time; when one gestured with the right hand, the other gestured with the left. The performance lasted almost two hours, and the mirror repetition continued throughout.

The play takes place in a studio where a film is being made. The Director of the film and his crew are waiting for the Star, who is late. (On the program and in the dialogue, characters are referred to by position rather than by name.) They shoot a short sequence in which the Juvenile talks on a wall telephone. The pictures taken simultaneously by the two television cameras involved in the action appear on two television monitors suspended high in the center between the risers.

The Star arrives and chats with her Stand-in Female and has her makeup applied by the Makeup Man. (The risers indicate her dressing room, where several scenes take place. When she sits in the adjustable chair, most of the spectators can see her reflection in one of the suspended mirrors.) The wall telephone unit is replaced by a door unit—flats are braced at an angle across opposite corners of the space—and the Director explains the lines and actions of the scene to the Star: she is returning to her hotel room, when, drunk, she drops the key, asks the passing Juvenile for help, and he opens the door for her. Although she has only a few simple lines, the Star cannot remember them.

Back in her dressing room, the Star telephones her doctor but cannot reach him. She undresses, stretches out on the table, and the Makeup Man gives her a massage.

When the Director again attempts to shoot the scene, the Star becomes enraged because of the camera angle and walks off the set. After a conversation in her dressing room with the Stand-In Female and another call to her doctor in which he attempts to calm her, she attempts to seduce the Gaffer, who is the last one on the set. She has him undress and pose, lying on a red cloth. (His positions, also seen on the television monitors, and the background are intended to remind one of Marilyn Monroe's famous nude calendar photograph.) But then she asks him to dress, and he leaves.

The last segment of *The Marilyn Project* appears only on the two monitors. It is a short film sequence from the end of *Bus Stop*, starring Marilyn Monroe.

If we consider structure to be connections between the parts of a whole—the dynamics that hold it together—*The Marilyn Project* emphasized structure not usually found in drama. Most of this structure was spatial or three-dimensional; durationally it existed in the present moment rather than in extended time. At each moment of the performance, the spectator could select and make a myriad of comparisons across space. One could compare the movements and intonations of the paired performers. Sometimes they were identical, or almost so. Sometimes one or the other was, unintentionally, a second or so later than their alter egos The intent was to be in synchronization. The performers knew, however, that this would not always be possible. Schechner has explained how this worked.

During rehearsals I told the performers many times that although they should always try to be in synch inevitably during each performance they would get out of synch many times. The rule was for the person or team ahead to stop as soon as she/they were conscious of the divergence and let the other side catch up. Thus a musical structure, a kind of modified round, was inherent in the performance. There was no need to plan when these rounds would occur—they were random, but inevitable. I was pleased that in an environment that appeared to be so totally "controlled" a strong chance element was also there.

At the same time both I and the performers were aware of the emotional ramifications of this method. If a particularly moving speech was being spoken, and suddenly a silence developed where only one speaker was heard for several words, or a sentence; or a scene in which one side of the room became still, a kind of emptiness descended on the lines; or an echo-effect happened which is very different emotionally from the chorus-effect of most of the performance. This out-of-synch-followed-by-one-person-speaking even created feeling in scenes where feelings were unexpected: a definite focus replaced business at those moments. And during the fight between the Star and the Director the very different kinds of acting done by Joan MacIntosh—Ron Vawter on one side and Elizabeth LeCompte—Robert Fuhrman on the other was made even more different during rehearsals. Fuhrman got louder, Vawter quieter; MacIntosh often would shed tears, LeCompte rarely wept. When the Star stumbles back to her dressing room, the two performers were almost always out of synch—each performed the same gestures: taking a pill, getting out of costume, falling into the chair, reaching for the telephone, but these were done in very personal ways: clearly the audience was being offered differing interpretations of the same role and scene. Far from trying to "correct" these differences, I let them happen. (*Drama Review*, December 1976)

The same movement performed by two people of different physiques might seem quite different; gestures and expressions might differ in a pair because of somewhat different characterizations. When images appeared on the two television monitors, they, too, could be compared. Although the attempt was made by each Cameraperson and group of actors to make the pictures identical, there were always differences. Perhaps one face appeared slightly larger within the frame; perhaps one actor grimaced a bit while the other did not. Differences were magnified or made more apparent by the medium and the juxtapositioning of the two screens. Comparisons could also be made between the images on the television monitors and the actors and properties producing them. Here were two views of the same thing separated spatially. In the same way, the mirror above the chairs produced other views of the persons seated in the chairs, allowing a multiplicity of visual connections to be made. Since two people were speaking simultaneously, the spectator was also free to listen to the voice of one while watching the movements of the other. An extremely complex web of visual and aural comparisons was created throughout the space, linking disparate points sometimes twenty-five or thirty feet apart.

Time or durational structure was primarily narrative: a sequence of events during one day's shooting of a film. But certain structural connections were made across time or through extended time by means of repetitions. A Bit Player was rehearsing her part: she had to walk into the scene and say one line. Over and over while other activity was going on, she repeated the action, trying it in various ways. The Star often stammered, repeating words or phrases several times. When the doctor asks her if she is happy at the studio, she says. "I . . . I . . . I . . . yes. I . . . I . . . yes." Some verbal echoes or connections are made across longer spans of time. When the Star drops her key, she says to the Juvenile, "Can you help me?" Later, when talking to the doctor and, still later, when seducing the Gaffer, she repeats the same phrase.

If we think of a Structuralist play as one that calls attention to or emphasizes its structural features, *The Marilyn Project* would be Structuralist.

There is, however, a more refined definition. We may say that in a Structuralist play structure is the most important, the dominant thing. Is structure most important in *The Marilyn Project?*

If meaning is most important, structure will have or create meaning. If structure does not create meaning, meaning cannot be more important unless it is strengthened by other elements. What is the relation of the unusual structures of *The Marilyn Project* to meaning?

Of course, the stammering of the Star is primarily characterization. It is intended to tell us something about her mental and emotional state. Any structural considerations are secondary.

The repetition of "Can you help me?" draws our attention to the phrase and underlines it so that it carries more meaning than it would in the context of each scene alone. It becomes thematic, seeming to point to what the play is "really about."

The Bit Player who practices her single line over and over also seems to be telling about the theme of the play, its deeper meaning, rather than merely rehearsing. They—for, of course, there are two Bit Players— become a chorus, emphasizing meaning. The sentence they repeat and repeat almost throughout the play is, "She's just the kind of girl who always gets in trouble." (In part, this repetition also can be seen as the extended preparation for a joke. When the Bit Player finally gets to perform, she says ". . . gets into trouble" and has to be corrected by the Director.)

These uses of repetition for characterization, emphasis, and humor are not primarily structural. Nor are they particularly unusual. But what about the unusual staging with a double cast? Is meaning most important here?

Perhaps it is a huge metaphor. Stage designers often work meta-phorically—making a setting for *The Balcony,* for example, out of large mirrors—and the duplication itself may have meaning. Since one cast is a mirror image of the other, it could be considered a statement about the Star's "living in a world of mirrors." The fact that the Makeup Man works on her more than once in the play, her concern about her appearance, a hand mirror that she uses, even the mirrors hanging above her makeup chair, would reinforce this.

Of course, there could be other intellectual interpretations of the double structure. Anything can be interpreted. Again, meaning would be the most important thing.

There are certain facts about *The Marilyn Project,* however, that tend to decrease the importance of its meaning and to emphasize the impor-tance of its structure. Like a scenic metaphor, the metaphor (if that is what it is) of mirror casts does not change and develop. At some point, probably quite early in the performance, we "understand" it. Our under-standing does not change, although the experience may become more intense as it extends in time. There is no new information to be gained from it. The spectators do not even need to watch both casts; all the in-formation may be obtained by following only one. Yet if the spectators want to make detailed comparisons, they can be very busy. These com-parisons of voices, images, gestures, characterizations have nothing to do with meaning. They do not clarify or expand the basic metaphor, if one exists. If one is concerned with meaning, the complexity of the double staging probably would be, as a reviewer said, "not a deepening but a distraction."

Because of the density of sensory comparisons, the spectators' per-ceptual mechanism could be heavily and actively involved in the present moment. This, of course, would not rule out intellectual involvement with the ideas, message, and literal content of the play, but there does seem to be a general inverse relationship between the two types of functioning. If so, the concrete "thereness" of the sensory involvement in the present moment worked against meaning and made structure more important.

Of course, the characterization of the actors—one of the ways in which they gave meaning to the play—was affected by the problem of staying in synchronization with a frequently unseen and distant "part-ner." The actors' behavior was obviously bound and restricted by the structure. Their spontaneity was not as complete as it might have been in another acting context, although the relationship between freedom and control shifted and at times—when, for example, intense emotion was called for—was more obvious than at others. At any rate, the double/simultaneous structure of *The Marilyn Project* production made technical demands on the actors that tended to work against (or were at least unrelated to) meaning. One could see both characterization and technical performing in the actors' work.

Nor was the duplication of the two casts exactly identical. One Cameraperson was a woman and the other a man. The Telephone Voice that spoke to the Star for the doctor and others came from a man and a woman seated on a platform directly across from the television monitors. If one were not expected to compare in detail the differences between the two casts, there would be no point to these obvious differences—differences that, in themselves, had no meaning.

In the discussion period that followed a performance for the Director's Unit, Schechner was asked if the double casts were created specifically for Gaard's script or if it could have been any script. He said that it could have been any script; the script did not matter. Another playscript on a different subject would have given up the repetition typical of shooting a film: the ritual of numerous "takes," the lines and actions repeated and repeated. It would have given up the Stand-In Female, who was dressed and made up exactly like the Star. The basic formal structures would exist, however, in a similar production of any script.

If theatrical Structuralism is defined as the primacy of performance structure rather than meaning, it is probably most accurate to say that for some *The Marilyn Project* was a Structuralist play; for others it was not. Like an optical illusion it could be seen either of two contradictory ways. One was not "correct" and the other "incorrect." How the production was seen—whether meaning or structure was dominant—depended upon habit and taste, among other things. Certainly, meaning was hard to avoid. Simple and obvious intellectual points were made over and over in a straightforward and even aggressive way. But for some people, at least, *The Marilyn Project* was a Structuralist play.

Double Gothic

"*Double Gothic*," the newspaper advertisements read, was "a Structuralist play by Michael Kirby." About twenty metal folding chairs have been arranged in three rows to face a huge, irregular, boxlike construction of shiny black plastic. The side of the construction that faces them is a rectangular wall of black scrim about eighteen feet wide and eight feet high.

The scrim is blank; nothing can be seen behind it. Perhaps the spectators notice from the programs they have been given that only women will act in *Double Gothic:* Anne Fox, Amy Heebner, Brigette Kueppers, Maria Myers, Marguerite Oerlemans, and Ela Troyano. (Mark Daniels is listed as assistant manager, Suzanne Pillsbury as sound, and Allan Pierce as house manager.)

The lights go out. Loud recorded electronic music is heard. It sounds somewhat like organ music: deep, sustained, droning sounds. For quite a while, there is only total darkness and the lugubrious music.

The music stops abruptly, and a light comes on. It hangs somewhere behind the black scrim wall. We see a woman hobbling on one foot. "My shoe is broken," she says. Almost before she has finished, the light has gone out, and the music has returned.

Again the spectators sit in the dark for a while. Suddenly the music stops again, and another light comes on at a different spot behind the scrim. In the cone of white light under the hanging bulb, we see another woman. She points at something and says simply. "Your shoelace is un-tied." The light goes out, and the music comes on again.

Music and darkness continue to be interrupted by brief illuminated actions that appear for only a couple of seconds. The lights hang above the heads of the performers, their conical shapes casting pools of light downward. There is no way of predicting where within the shrouded box the next light will go on. Sometimes the actress who appears in the light speaks; sometimes she merely performs a brief silent action. Some of the figures seem very dim, at a great distance away; others are clearer, but all are made hazy by the scrim.

Perhaps the spectator notices that the early actions and the spoken phrases relate to shoes, to feet. A woman holding a doll says, "One of her shoes is missing." A seated woman slowly takes off one of her stock-ings. A woman in a white laboratory coat stands looking at a high-heeled woman's shoe she holds in her hand. Later, as the intervals of darkness and music grow shorter and shorter, there are images of gloves, of hands. "Is that a wedding ring?" one of the women asks. The woman in the white lab coat takes off rubber gloves. A seated woman admires her fingernails and asks, "Are they long enough?" For the first time, three lights come on simultaneously. They hang close to the spectators at equal intervals, lighting a narrow corridor behind the black scrim. The rear wall of the corridor, about four feet back, is another scrim. We cannot see behind it because the only light is between the two scrims.

A young woman puts down a suitcase and looks around. There is the sound of a passing car, and she waves futilely. She sits on the suitcase, examining one of her shoes, which is broken. Another car passes; again she waves without success. Another woman has appeared at the left. She wears men's clothing, carries a lantern, and has one arm in a sling, the hand bandaged. "Hello," the first woman says, "I had an accident. I must have gone to sleep at the wheel." She laughs. The other woman stares at her silently. "Do you live around here?" the first woman asks. The woman with the lantern steps forward, holding out a piece of paper. "Is that for me?" the first woman asks, limping as she walks on one shoe. "My shoe is broken."

The acting is simple, clear, quiet, unhurried. It appears that the woman with her arm in a sling is a deaf mute; she cannot speak, but she seems to understand something of what is said. Perhaps she can read lips. The paper she gives the woman who had an accident is an invitation, apparently an offer of refuge for the night. She accepts, taking off her glove to shake hands, but when she turns for her suitcase, it has disappeared. Lightning flashes and thunder sounds as the young woman follows the mute woman off.

After another brief interval of darkness and music, a row of three lights at some distance from the audience goes on. They, too, illuminate a narrow corridor parallel to the front wall of the black box. The figure who appears seems distant and faint. A young woman with a shoulder bag puts down a suitcase. She puts up the umbrella she carries and looks around. A dog howls in the distance. As she folds the umbrella again, she seems to see someone. A second woman—wearing a coat, cap, and dark glasses and using a stick as a cane—is standing silently at the right. "Do you know what time it is?" the first woman asks. "The train was late." "Are you Ela?" the woman with the cane says. "Yes, I am." The young woman steps forward to shake hands. "That's nice. I thought nobody had come to meet me." We have difficulty seeing the actors clearly; it is not easy to hear their quiet voices. The woman with the cane does not take the extended hand; apparently, she is blind. "The doctor" has sent her. "Is it far to the hospital?" the young woman asks. "To the retreat," the other—who has introduced herself as Marguerite—replies, "It's across the tracks and through the woods a way." "Wait," says the young woman as they are about to set out, "Your shoelace is untied. I'll do it." There is lightning and thunder as they leave.

The three lights that come on next are farther away than the ones that lit the scene of the accident but closer than the ones that lit the meeting at the rural railroad station. The action in the corridor they illuminate is dimmer than that of the first scene but clearer than that of the second. (The space created by the several parallel walls of scrim was ambiguous.

It was difficult to tell how many scrims were involved. One critic wrote that there were "approximately eight corridors divided by longitudinal panels of gauze." Actually, there were six scrim walls, which created five four-foot-wide corridors parallel to the front plane. Watching the woman hobble on one shoe, the spectators looked through one scrim; watching the woman with the umbrella, they looked through five scrim walls. Now we are looking through two walls of black scrim.) The mute woman appears alone and steps up on a low black platform at the right, apparently signaling to someone with the lantern. The young woman arrives. "Don't go so fast," she pleads. When the young woman sits, the mute woman disappears. The young woman is left alone. Finally, the mute appears again and points to something in the distance. "Is that the house?" the young woman asks. The mute confirms it with a nod and guttural sounds. As they are about to continue, the young woman sees something on the ground and pulls away in fear, pointing at it. With help, the mute pulls a glove on her unbandaged hand and, with a sudden lunge, holds up a large snake. She puts it out of the way, and the two women go off again into the darkness.

Now we return to the two women who were going "through the woods a way." They can be seen and heard more clearly than before, but they are farther away than the scene we have just watched. (They are in the fourth corridor; previously they had met in the fifth.) After brushing cobwebs away from her face, the younger woman sees something on the ground. It is a female doll. When the young woman sits on a low black platform at the left to change into her boots, the blind woman disappears. The young woman is left alone. When the blind woman appears again, the young woman, not thinking, points to something in the distance and asks, "Is that the house?" "Over there?" replies the blind woman, pointing with her cane. As the two go off, the lights go out.

The third scene involving the young woman whose car ran off the road is played farther away and is less clearly seen than the first two scenes of that story. (It is in the third or middle corridor; the spectators are looking through three scrim walls.) Arriving at her destination, the young woman is greeted by a woman in a wheelchair, who communicates with the mute in sign language. Outside, a thunderstorm rages. The mute, whose name is Brigitte, appears with a pan of water, and, on signaled orders from the woman in the wheelchair, somewhat forcibly washes the young woman's feet.

The third scene in the story of the young woman going to the "retreat" is played in the same corridor and has the same visibility as the scene we have just watched. (Because the usual interval of droning electronic music in the darkness divides the two scenes, some spectators may not have been aware that the same space was used.) We hear thunder; a storm is raging outside. The lights flicker, and a woman in a white laboratory coat takes off her rubber gloves. The young woman, who has left her shoes in the vestibule, thanks the doctor for waiting and comments, "It's such a long shot." "She may be here," the doctor answers. The doctor limps when she walks. The blind woman appears with some slippers, and, sitting, the young woman takes off her stockings. As the doctor kneels, putting the slippers on her visitor's feet, the light flickers again.

When a row of three hanging lights comes on again, it is dimmer and farther away from us. (It is the fourth corridor, where the young woman on her way to the "retreat" discovered the doll. The platform at the left has become a bed; it is covered with a sheet and blanket and has a pillow.) The woman in the wheelchair shows her guest where she is to sleep. When the young woman turns back the bedcovers, she gasps, "What is it, my dear?" The young woman puts on one of her gloves, makes a quick lunge under the bedcovers, and holds up a large snake. When the woman in the wheelchair is wheeled out, the young woman searches the room, looking carefully in all the corners. Satisfied, she begins to undress for bed. She is in her slip. Sitting on the bed, she puts out the lamp, and the light goes out.

Now the corridor that is lit is closer, and the actors can be heard and seen more clearly. (It is the same space in which the young woman who had an accident traveled through the forest. The platform at the right has become a bed with sheet, blanket, and pillow.) The doctor is showing her visitor to the room where she is to sleep. When the guest turns down the covers to her bed, she discovers the doll. "Isn't that cute! She's sleeping." The doctor takes the doll and looks at it. "I found her," the young woman explains. "She was wearing clothes then. Now she's ready for bed." As the blind woman is leaving, she tells the young woman to lock her door at once. Alone, the young woman locks her door and gets undressed. She is sitting on her bed in her slip. She puts out the candles in the candelabra, and the lights go out.

The lights that come on at the far side of the space are seen only dimly. The woman we have seen in the wheelchair sits at a small table putting on false fingernails. Brigitte, the mute, enters. Her hand is no longer bandaged. She accuses the seated woman, and an argument develops: "You don't care about the old ones. . . . It's the new ones you're excited about!" "You bitch!" says the other woman, standing up. "You tried to kill her, didn't you?" She points. "You and your snakes!" The mistress of the house accuses her "mute" assistant of being ungrateful for having her hand "fixed." After some accord is reached, the "mute" asks the other woman if she is "going in there tonight." "I might," the "cripple" replies. "I think I will. Do you want to watch? You can watch through the painting."

The light goes on in the corridor closest to the audience. The doctor is sitting at a small table in a dressing gown. When the blind woman enters, the doctor suggests that the groping gesture her associate sometimes uses to find her way is not realistic. The "blind" woman can actually see. An argument flares. The "blind" woman accuses the doctor of going "downstairs" while she was away: "I heard someone screaming, too." When they are reconciled, the doctor says, "I have an idea." "Tell me about it." "I'd rather not." A dispute begins again. "Why don't you watch?" taunts the doctor. "You can watch through the mirror."

The corridor between the scrim walls where the young woman whose car ran off the road has remained in bed is illuminated. (It is the fourth corridor away from the spectators.) The young woman sits up suddenly. Apparently she has heard something. The "mute" woman enters, and they have a brief, hurried conversation. "You can't stay here," says the "mute." "It's dangerous for you. . . . It would be better in the woods." "What kind of danger?" the young woman replies. "I'm not going to run away, if that's what you mean. I want to know what's going on here." The "mute" leaves abruptly, and the lights got out.

Now, the "bedroom" where the other young woman is asleep (the second corridor) is lit. She seems to hear something and sits up. "Who is it? Who's there?" The "blind" woman enters and tells her to leave. The dialogue is exactly the same as in the preceding scene. "I'm not going to run away, if that's what you mean. I want to know what's going on here." "Please," urges the "blind" woman, "I can't talk now. I have to go." She disappears, and the lights go out.

The loud, organlike electronic music swells in the darkness. For the first time, lights appear simultaneously in two different corridors. The young woman closest to us has turned on the candelabra, and the other young woman has lit the lamp with the glass chimney. Somewhat dim, these lights are the only illumination. Holding the lamp and candelabra, the two women begin to walk slowly through the corridors in their white slips, exploring the space. Lightning flashes. The music drones and rumbles. Vague blurs in darkness, the women weave their way between the scrims. Now both of the women have disappeared. Nothing can be seen in the darkness of the scrim box. Only the loud, surging music remains.

After a few moments, the music stops suddenly, and a single hanging light comes on briefly. In it we see the "crippled" woman standing and pointing, as we saw her do in the argument. "You tried to kill her," she says. The light goes out, and the music continues. After about five seconds, the music and darkness are broken again by a single light at another spot in the construction. The "blind" woman is pointing, as she did not long ago. The lights go out. As at the opening of the play, we see a series of images appearing briefly at unpredictable places in the space. Now we may recognize them. They all occurred in the scenes and are presented at those same places. (In like manner, we may have recognized some of the actions and lines from the opening sequence when they later occurred in the same locations during the scenes.) Now pointing recurs in the images. "My suitcase!" exclaims one young woman, pointing. "There's a star," says the other young woman; she points. The intervals of darkness and music are growing longer. We have to wait longer and longer before the next brief glow of light appears. Now two people are together in the light; one hands something to the other. The "crippled" woman hands eyeglasses to the "mute" and orders, "Put them on." The light goes out. The doctor gives something to her visitor: "Here's the key." The light goes out. The blind woman hands a lily to her companion: "Look, I brought you this." The light goes out. Now the intervals of darkness and music are quite long, almost thirty seconds. The images revealed by the brief spots of illumination are from the first scenes of the play. The mute woman hands a piece of paper to the young woman whose car went off the road. The light goes out. The blind woman hands a flashlight to the young woman she has come to meet. The light goes out. The music and darkness continue, but no more lights come on. Finally, the music fades; the house lights come on. *Double Gothic* is over.

When there was applause from the other side of the huge plastic-and-scrim construction, some spectators realized for the first time that an audience had also been watching the play from that side. In the dim light and confusion of entering, it was possible not to notice that people were being seated in two sections, one on either side of the black box. Spectators could not see through the front scrim wall when the house light illuminated their side of it, and they could not see through the rear wall—the sixth scrim—during the play because there was no light on the spectators behind it.

Thus two audiences watched the play at the same time, looking at each other without seeing each other. The scenes that have been described as being close to one audience were actually far from the other.

What one audience could see and hear clearly was dim and faint to the other, and vice versa. For each audience, the two stories passed through each other. The story that began close to the spectators moved progressively farther away, and the story that began in the distance moved progressively closer.

The primary durational or time structures of *Double Gothic* developed from reading *Morphology of the Folktale* by Vladimir Propp. Propp posits that all Russian fairy tales are composed of variations on a limited number of events. None of these events are obligatory, but those that are used must occur in a particular order. This concept turns one's attention to the event-structure underlying any genre of literature or drama. We may hypothesize that any genre makes use of a limited number of events and that these occur in a particular order. This is one of the characteristics that distinguish the individual work as part of a genre and identify the genre itself. Even if this theory were not true, the concept could provide the basis on which to construct a Structuralist play such as *Double Gothic*. In art, ideas do not have to be correct or true to be useful.

The second useful concept found in Propp is what he calls character "function." Propp explains function as "an act of character, defined from the point of view of its significance for the course of the action." In other words, characters are considered not in terms of their unique, individual, idiosyncratic personalities, but of how they function, how they relate to the story. In personality, the hero in one story may be quite different from the hero in another, but they both function as heroes. Although psychological and situational variations are infinite, the number of character functions is limited.

To work with event-structure, I needed to use more than one story. A single story, even though it was developed through an analysis of event-structure, would merely embody that structure. Everything has structure, and the structure of the particular sequence of events in a single story would not attract attention to itself, rise to visibility, or be dynamic. If more than one story was told, however, and these stories, although superficially different, had the same event-structure, that structure would become visible, a thing itself, dominant.

When I first started working with Propp's concepts, I began to write a play in a genre other than the Gothic. After all, the genre itself was unimportant. I began to write *The Morphology of Science Fiction*. It presented three simultaneous stories that were identical in their event-structure but entirely different in the ways the events were embodied.

One story was set in an underwater kingdom, one in a hidden city in the Andes, one on and near a moon of Mars (water/earth/air). The heroes of the three stories were a woman, an android, and a man. Thus three versions of the "same" event—unlike, of course, in all their superficial details of location, situation, and personality—were to be seen at the same time, side by side. The three stories, composed of the same number of "identical" events, would begin and end simultaneously. The writing seemed to go well, but I soon realized that to have dialogue that did not overlap, at least two-thirds of each individual scene had to be in wordless action. This condition, in itself, was not a problem. I have intentionally written plays that were primarily visual and had little speaking. But the visuals became very complicated and prohibitively expensive. I set the project aside.

Double Gothic was a more practical development of these ideas, using a different genre. Two stories having the same event-structure would be enough to demonstrate that structure, to make it manifest. I decided to alternate two stories—playing a scene from one and then the "same" scene from the other—rather than to present them simultaneously.

In rehearsal, one story was set to play at one side of the black box and the other story at the other side. One story was to be in the foreground and the other in the background for each of the two audiences. When we moved into the construction itself, one of the actresses, Ela Troyano, pointed out that the stories could be presented so that they began at opposite sides of the box and progressed scene by scene, corridor by corridor, to the opposite side, thus passing through each other. This is what we did. The movement of each of the stories away from one audience and toward the other audience—the clarity and visibility of the scenes controlled by the number of intervening scrim walls—was a purely formal structure. It had nothing to do with meaning or message.

Alternating the stories added the dynamic of anticipation. Once the spectator realized that the second story was a version of the first, certain elements could be expected. This feature related to the comparatively low visibility and audibility in the distant corridors. What was not available to the eyes and ears might be filled in, to some extent, by the mind and imagination. If anything was not perceived because of darkness, low vocal level, and intervening scrim walls, it could be assumed to be similar to what was perceived clearly in the corresponding close scene.

Character functions were kept to a minimum. Each story had a Heroine, an Antagonist, and a Helper of the Antagonist. The decision to use all women was completely arbitrary. (I am fond of such decisions.) My preceding play, *Identity Control,* had had only men in the roles. Why not use only women in *Double Gothic*? Of course, a handsome mysterious man is a standard feature of the Gothic genre, and repressed sexuality is one of its dominant characteristics. After one performance, I was asked why I had put lesbian material into the play. The answer was that sex was vital for the Gothic genre, and I had chosen to do one (or two) version(s) with only women. This incident, to me, is an example of how structuralist thinking can create unusual combinations of elements that would not be produced by following the usual creative methods of message, intuition, inspiration, and taste.

structuralist film

Many structuralist plays could be made directly into structuralist films. The time or durational structures of the live performances could simply be filmed, with or without the filter of changed camera angle and variation of frame size, to make a movie. Even the three-dimensional spatial structures important to most structuralist plays could be represented or "translated" in film. (For example, two alternating and interwoven stories separated spatially on stage could be distinguished in a film by using different color filters for each; spatial progressions could be translated into color progressions, and so on.) Yet it would be impossible to make most structuralist films into live performances. Structuralist films tend to exploit the high degree of mechanical control inherent in the medium, a control that is not possible in live performance. Thus an analysis of selected films that may be called structuralist should tell us something about the media of film and theatre and about Structuralism itself.

Like live performance, film may be analyzed in terms of both durational or time structures and of nondurational structures of the present moment. Nondurational structures in theatre are both two-dimensional (the picture-frame stage) and three-dimensional, relating to both painting and sculpture. The fundamental two-dimensional character of the projected film image and its representation, rather than embodiment, of three-dimensional space relate it, of course, much more closely to the structural possibilities of painting. Two facts tend to modify this overly simple schematization: (1) even in painting, it takes time to "read" two-dimensional structure, and (2) durational and nondurational structures are reference points on a conceptual continuum rather than mutually exclusive categories; in film much more than in painting, there are structures that involve time to a limited extent and yet may be considered most productively in terms of the present moment.

Clear examples of structuring of the present moment in film can be found in *Frame* and *Picking Up the Pieces* by Ken Kobland. The first section of *Picking Up the Pieces* (1978) is a sequence of seventeen or eighteen still color photographs, all taken in the same entrance hallway of an old but clean tenement building. No people are visible. The even intervals of the stairs, the patterns of the tile floor, the strip of molding halfway up the wall, the verticals of the walls that enclose the narrow space produce pictures with clear, precise lines and angles; all are similar, all have the same colors and forms, all are related to each other.

The second sequence begins with the same picture that began the first sequence. Now the rectangular center section seems to have been cut out and replaced: a line distinguishes the center from the rest of the picture. As the sequence continues, presenting the photographs fairly quickly in their previous order, this center section of the first picture appears in the center of each of the others. The colors and qualities of central and surrounding images are the same. The compositions are sometimes closely related, sometimes quite different.

When the third sequence of *Picking Up the Pieces* begins, the rectangular center portion of one of the other pictures is seen briefly superimposed in the center of the first picture. In a moment, we find that it belongs to the second picture; it fits when it is presented there. Then it appears centered in order on each of the other pictures of the sequence.

This progression continues. The center rectangular portion of each of the pictures appears centered in turn on each of the pictures in the sequence. Once in each repetition—when the center picture is superimposed on the picture from which it was taken—the overall picture is complete rather than contradictory. This format emphasizes the comparison of the part to the whole, the relationship—congruity, similarity, or difference—between the central image and the surrounding image in a two-dimensional field. This is structure in the present moment.

The repetition of images and the orderly sequence also bring in the time dimension. We anticipate the length of each sequence. We begin to expect the moment when a central picture will become congruent. Since the order is always the same, we anticipate that when the center of the last picture in the series appears, the final sequence has begun; when it is superimposed on the last picture, making a complete image, the film will end. Thus, although two-dimensional structures are predominant, durational structures involving memory, expectancy, repetition, and patterning are also important.

Frame (1977), actually made by Kobland before *Picking Up the Pieces*, uses the same image-within-an-image format but with moving pictures. All of the footage for *Frame* was shot from inside a car moving along a road lined with beach cottages. The cottages are not occupied; no people can be seen. In some shots, the camera points straight ahead; in others, it is aimed directly to the left, where sand and water may be glimpsed behind the row of small wooden houses moving past. The film itself is composed of several sequences, in each of which one shot is inserted within another. In each, a rectangular picture having the same proportions as the main picture is placed in the center of the main picture. The larger motion picture makes a thick rectangular frame around the smaller picture in its center. Thus the "content" of *Frame* becomes the relationship—more or less in the present moment—between the two moving pictures. A subtitle printed on the film explains the relationship in each sequence between the frame picture and the picture in its center. The caption of the first sequence reads, "The inner image is delayed." In both shots, the camera is pointing through the front window of the moving car. In fact, there are not two different shots but one: the moving picture in the center is the same as that of the frame, but it is printed "out of sync." What we see first in the frame we see a moment later in the center. When, at the end of the shot, the frame goes black, the inner picture continues a moment longer. Other sequences present other relationships between the inner and outer pictures: the two images are simultaneous, the inner image precedes the outer one, one of the images is reversed, the inner shot is taken to the side and in the outer one the camera looks ahead, the outer moves at twice the speed of the inner and the cottages move in opposite directions, and so forth. In each of these relationships, the emphasis, as in *Picking Up the Pieces,* is on the relationship between parts of a two-dimensional field. The main structuring exists in the present moment.

To make the comparison as specific and accurate as possible, however, the mind/eye attempts to capture specific information from the flow of images through time—to establish particular, if fleeting, reference points and relationships in time so as to verify and perceptually establish the correspondences announced in the titles. (Absence of titles would not eliminate this structural activity; it would merely provoke a wider and more intense search for the nature of the visual comparison.) In the first sequence, for example, when the images are the same but the inner one precedes the outer, the spectator attempts to remember one particular house or detail and to recognize it again when it appears a moment later in the moving outer image. Because of the speed of the car, the plainness of the landscape, and the similarity of the beach cottages, this is not easy. Yet to the extent that it can be done, the precise time discrepancy between the images can be established intellectually. Thus relationships in time—fourth-dimensional structures—of a fixed and limited duration also become important in a film that uses a two-dimensional format and emphasizes structure in the present moment.

Time structures—memory and expectancy of a different type and of much longer duration—are dominant in Ken Jacobs's *The Doctor's Dream*. Indeed, Jacobs's film, in emphasizing these structures for its own purposes, can be seen as demonstrative of how memory and expectancy function in the traditional narrative movie. These are the first ten shots of *The Doctor's Dream*:

1 Facing the camera, a middle-aged woman wearing a long dress stands on the porch of a wooden farmhouse. She looks worried as she takes down from the wall a horn made from a bull's horn and blows it.

2 Seated on a wagon filled with hay and pulled by two horses, a farmer and a young boy drive in from the right.

3 The woman we have seen on the porch is seated to the right of a young girl who is covered with blankets and obviously sick. The woman—we can assume she is the child's mother—is looking at a thermometer while she feels her daughter's forehead with the other hand.

4 The farmer and the boy—father and son—are seated on the wagon. "Carol Ann is worse," says the boy. "I know," his father answers. "Better get on Old Joe and ride for the doctor."

5 Extreme close-up of the thermometer: it reads 104.5 degrees.

6 The farmer and his son climb down from the wagon.

7 The mother takes the thermometer from the mouth of her daughter and looks at it.

8 The mother on the porch. She again blows the horn.

9 A desk with a microscope, books, and other items on it. Apparently it is a doctor's office in his house. An elderly man with a beard and wearing a dark suit—the doctor—steps in from the left and takes off his hat. A white-haired woman—his wife—appears. "Why, Jason!" she says. "What are you doing home?" The doctor has "a lot of work to do," his wife can help him, and he sits behind the desk, facing the camera, peering into the microscope. He is searching for a vaccine.

10 The farmer unhitches the harness that attaches the near horse to the wagon. He boosts his son onto the back of the horse. "Ride, boy, ride!"

The acting, sets, lighting, and camerawork indicate professional studio production. The film—apart from its fictional setting before the First World War—does not seem completely contemporary. Even without previous information, one might deduce that Jacobs did not shoot the footage for *The Doctor's Dream*. But although the material of the film seems to be that of a traditional narrative with clear characters, obvious relationships, and a simple situation, the order of the shots does not follow the traditional order. Even without being told, one might guess that Jacobs was reordering the shots of a film made by someone else. (When *The Doctor's Dream* was shown in 1979 at the Collective in New York, an announcement was made before the screening that Jacobs had rearranged, according to a particular system, a film made by someone else and had used every shot from the "found" film in his own work. Although there would be no way of knowing, merely from viewing Jacobs's film, that he had used all of the shots, one might assume it, once the pattern of rearrangement was understood.)

At any rate, the spectators might begin, very early in their viewing, to realize that the story was being told in a discontinuous way. Every other shot seems to move the narrative forward. And although the intervening shots do not add to this narrative, they involve the same people. More significantly, the intervening shots precede the events of the forward-moving story. Finally, the spectator realizes that the shots being presented between the shots of the forward-moving story are moving backward— they are being presented in reverse order, and each of these shots belongs before, rather than after, the shot before the last one. We are watching the same story going forward and backward in alternating shots at the same time. We can deduce that Jacobs began in the middle with his reordering and that the story will both begin and end at the end of the film.

This is exactly what Ken Jacobs did to make *The Doctor's Dream*. He began with a half-hour black-and-white narrative film made for television and reedited it to make his own film.

The original film opens with a shot of a genre painting in which a bearded doctor sits pensively and watchfully at the side of a sick girl while her parents wait nearby. The filmed action begins with the doctor being awakened in the early morning by a knock at the door; he looks at his watch. The doctor visits a farm, advising a middle-aged woman to "keep him in bed" as much as possible and let him (obviously her son, who is ill) play in the sun. Then the doctor visits another farm family—a father, mother, son, and daughter—taking as a present for the young girl a calf that he has received in payment. "This cow," he says, "is Carol Ann's." Rain threatens, and the doctor stays with the family briefly, reading to the girl from *Beauty and the Beast* and telling her about gold at the end of the rainbow that appears after the storm. The doctor leaves.

On the porch of his home, the doctor removes a bandage from the arm of a boy who has been his patient. In the farmhouse, the young girl, apparently stricken with the same disease that is affecting her neighbor, collapses. Using a microscope, the doctor searches for a vaccine. The mother takes the daughter's temperature, realizes that she is very sick, and signals with a horn to her husband and son, who are just returning on their wagon from work.

The son rides off on one of the horses to get the doctor. The doctor, meanwhile, discovers a vaccine he thinks might work. At the farm, he administers it to the sick girl. He and the family wait. The son goes onto the porch, where it is raining, and prays. The doctor administers the vaccine again. The crisis passes. The father goes to tell his son; the mother does "not know how to thank" the doctor. Later, the young girl is recovering. The doctor, whom she has not seen in a while, arrives and tells her of going to the city, where he has apparently achieved some fame because of developing the vaccine. He gives the girl some jewelry and drives off in his carriage.

Jacobs's rearrangement begins with the middle two shots of the original film and works alternately backward and forward shot by shot. (Or one might say, he began with the shot immediately before the exact middle of the original film and worked alternately forward and backward.) The new order is: the middle two shots, the shot that preceded them, the next shot after the middle ones, the second shot before the middle ones, the second shot after the middle ones, and so on. Thus the middle ten shots of the original film, given in Jacobs's order above, were, in their original order:

1 The doctor comes into his study and goes to work. (Shot number 9 in Jacobs's version.)

2 The mother takes the thermometer from her daughter's mouth and looks at it. (7)

3 The thermometer reads 104.5 degrees. (5)

4 Looking at the thermometer, the mother feels her daughter's forehead. (3)

5 On the porch, the woman blows a horn. (1)

6 The father and son arrive in the wagon. (2)

7 "Carol Ann is worse," says the son. The father tells the son he'd better ride for the doctor. (4)

8 They climb down from the wagon. (6)

9 The mother blows the horn again. (8)

10 The father helps his son onto the horse, and the boy rides off. (10)

Thus in Jacobs's version, the story folds back on itself. Shots of the doctor and the family waiting alternate with shots of the girl collapsing, the doctor removing the young boy's bandages, the doctor's discussion about the rainbow with the healthy young girl. A shot of the son on the porch in the rain is juxtaposed with one of the doctor with the calf. Recovering, unable to walk, Carol Ann sees the doctor in the forward-moving sequence, while in the reversed sequence she runs to greet him as he brings her the calf. The giving of the jewelry alternates with the doctor being awakened. The painting that opened the original film is the next to last shot in Jacobs's film; it is followed by the doctor's carriage driving away from the camera into the distance—the last shot in both films.

In watching the traditional narrative film, one forms certain expectations about what will be presented next. These expectations, which may be called structural because they involve the relationship between parts of the film, hold together by their presence extended sections of time and join one moment (when the expectancy is formed) with another (when the expectancy is either confirmed or denied). Some expectancies are about what will happen in the story: the son will reach the doctor in time, the doctor will discover a vaccine, Carol Ann will recover. These narrative expectancies are of various durations. In *The Doctor's Dream*, it is not long before we realize the son has told the doctor of his sister's sickness, but waiting to discover the efficacy of the vaccine lasts much longer. Expectancies of the shortest duration involve the information to be conveyed in the following shot or shot sequence. If a person looks at a thermometer, we may expect to learn momentarily, either visually or audially, what the temperature is. If a horn is blown as a signal, we expect a response (although this response may, of course, not be forthcoming), and whoever appears next on the screen is at least tentatively identified as the recipient of the message. Thus the structure of a film that tells a story can be seen in part as a series of narrative expectancies of different lengths, sometimes "nested" or placed one within another.

Expectancy in a narrative film, however, involves not only what will happen but how the information will be presented. If someone looks at a thermometer he or she is holding, we may expect the next shot to be a close-up of the thermometer. If a just-awakened man—the doctor in the opening moments of the original *Doctor's Dream*—reaches for his watch, we might expect the next shot to be a close-up of the watch. We may expect a long shot of a wagon to be followed by a medium shot of its occupants, and so forth. The way of telling a story in film has its own logic that engenders certain expectancies about technique.

Many expectancies in film are conscious, and our savoring of them is part of the dramatic excitement, but many are nonconscious or pre-conscious. From our first film experience, we begin to establish both conscious and nonconscious mental systems for predicting accurately what will occur next. Certain bits of information, certain constellations of facts, about both storytelling and the use of the medium are taken as indicators of what the future will bring. Filmmakers, too, are ingrained with these systems and patterns of prediction; they use them in creating their films. Tradition implies shared standards and assumptions, and the more traditional the film narrative, the more expectancy will play a part if the spectator belongs to that tradition.

In *The Doctor's Dream,* Jacobs exploits, puts pressure upon, and brings to conscious awareness the traditional mechanisms of expectancy structure. Let us ignore, for the moment, the interspersed shots of the backward-moving half of the narrative. Intercut black leader would func-tion to some extent in the same way. The forward-moving narrative is delayed, slowed; the time before expectancies are confirmed or denied is increased. Facts must be retained longer. The mind must carry and retain information and expectancies in an unusual, nonhabitual way. What was automatic and unconscious in the traditional arrangement of shots may now be forced into consciousness in an attempt to make sense out of the new, more difficult arrangement. It is not that structure did not exist in the traditional film, but the new, extended version of that struc-ture in the forward-moving portion of Jacobs's new film heightens it, makes it more intense. Attention is called to it, and it is made of primary aesthetic importance.

Knowing that the next shot in the narrative sequence will not arrive immediately forces the mind to make conscious decisions and con-sciously to store information when it could ordinarily work on a more spontaneous and unconscious level. But, of course, the intervening seg-ments in *The Doctor's Dream* are not black leader. They are shots involv-ing the same characters and locations as the forward-moving narrative. They function, in part, as "static," making the selection and combination of information, the focusing and retention of expectancies that much more difficult. This technique, too, is apt to force the work to a conscious level, emphasizing dynamic structure rather than narrative content and meaning. Extension, stretching, and heightening of normal expectancies become intellectual structural emotions in Jacobs's film.

The backward-moving half of the narrative achieves somewhat the same effect in a more complicated way. We have learned to predict what will follow the present moment we are watching in a film. We have not learned to predict what preceded it in an unknown past. All of our expectancy experience and habits of narration are aimed in one direction. When Jacobs forces us to ask, "What came before this shot, this scene?" rather than, "What will come after it?" the mechanisms of expectancy are again emphasized and made conscious. Although the same patterns of rearrangement—beginning in the middle and alternating forward-moving and backward-moving shot sequences—could be applied to any film, the effects would not necessarily be the same. A film without a clear, simple story line—a travelogue, say, or a poetic and impressionistic avant-garde piece—would not have the same dynamics, the same coherence, when rearranged. Length, too, would significantly affect the result, and if the halves of a feature-length film were intercut with each other, the resulting film might not have the clarity of Jacobs's *The Doctor's Dream*, which is based on a simple, obvious, compact narrative. By using and rearranging a half-hour film with many traditional literary/theatrical characteristics and intentions, Jacobs demonstrates in *The Doctor's Dream* that a structuralist film is "about" structure itself, "about" certain workings of the spectator's mind. It is not about its subject matter, it is not an interpretation of life or a statement about the world, it does not convey a message, and so forth. Jacobs expects the disassembled parts of the original film to be reassembled in the mind of the spectator. It is this process, this activity, that is important rather than the story, characterization, and moralizing that still remain in traces from the original film. The original narrative is exploited for its structural possibilities and nothing else.

In Ken Kobland's *Frame* and *Picking Up the Pieces*, we can also see the nontraditional relation of structuralist thought to subject matter. Subject matter exists in Kobland's films. They are films *of* something; they are not totally abstract or nonobjective. Yet, like Jacobs's *The Doctor's Dream*, they do not comment upon the subject matter, send messages about or through it, or elucidate it in any way. The road lined with beach houses that appears in *Frame* was chosen for its formal characteristics. The road is straight and smooth, its image clarifying the orientation of the shots, and its surface providing even transit for the camera. The almost identical beach houses lining the road at almost equal intervals serve as markers, indicating by the rhythm of their passing the speed of the camera/car and decreasing the possibility of finding quickly recognizable reference points. The entranceway of the tenement in *Picking Up the Pieces* provides clear, distinct, geometric patterns with consistent color, texture, and characteristics. The films are not about a beach road or a tenement entranceway; they exploit the characteristics of these subjects to emphasize the structures of the films, the relationships to be perceived in the subject material.

It does not matter that certain spectators do not perceive the structures, do not perform the "suggested" mental activities. All art is subjective. It lies, ultimately, in the personal experience of the observer. Therefore, no type or work of art receives the same response from everyone. That some people see little or nothing in these Structuralist films while others are very involved with them and deeply appreciate this involvement means nothing—other than being descriptive of the individual spectators. No artist, particularly an innovative artist, can expect a universal response to his work.

The films of both Kobland and Jacobs make use of techniques inherent in the medium. They could not be transferred, other than in the most general way and with different aesthetic results, into live performance. In part, *Frame* depends not merely on the comparison of one scene with a similar scene but on the comparison of a scene with itself. In part, it depends on the mechanically controlled, exact rate at which a scene is presented: one image moves twice as fast as another, and so on. In part, the image is altered mechanically—it appears reversed, creating a comparison that shifts attention away from the similarity/dissimilarity of detail. None of these structural effects would be possible with the same precision working with live actors on stage. Of course, in attempting to emulate *The Doctor's Dream,* a one-act play or a scene done on stage could be cut in half, divided into units, and acted with forward- and backward-moving sequences alternated. Even if the technical problems of joining the units could be solved—blackouts between each unit, for example, replacing the film cuts and concealing the movement of the actors—an actor, even with extensive rehearsal, could not be expected to act an emotion backward. He could not cut off the character's emotion when one unit ended and then, in a moment, present the feelings that preceded, led to, and developed into, those emotions. Although many of the external details of the rearranged narrative could be presented, they would not approximate the effects obtained in cutting and editing film. It is in the area available only to film that the structural concerns of Jacobs and Kobland lie.

Structuralist films are quite different from what have been called "structural" films. Structural films emphasize the overall form, shape, outline, or configuration, particularly through the use of a single extended shot or a minimal number of shots. Structuralist films emphasize internal relationships, correspondences, and differences, usually in a complex way. Structural films call attention to qualities and properties of the film.

Structuralist films call attention to the way the observer's mind works when viewing the film.

Because structuralist films involve both strictly calculated manipulations of their content and an emphasis on the thought processes of the spectator, some critics refer to them as "academic." This is intended negatively—referring, one supposes, to logical constructions and to the so-called ivory tower, where ideas are detached from the "real world." Ignoring the value judgment as merely an attempt to objectify the critic's personal taste (after all, some also use "critic" as a pejorative term), one can see the basis for this distinction. In composition, Structuralism does make use of logical thought. Some critics may prefer the illogicalities of intuition, inspiration, and personal idiosyncrasy—the traditional bases for creation. They are unable to recognize these factors when they appear—as they do—in Structuralism. Traditionally, thinking is evaluated to a great extent by the "importance" and "relevance" of its subject matter. Structuralism detaches thought processes from the subject matter of that thought. Some critics do not want to think in new ways with new priorities; they do not realize that abstract thought—the solution of a pure problem in, say, geometry or algebra—can produce powerful positive feelings and even a sense of usefulness. The thing need not always precede the thought. If we think in new ways, we will develop new things.

index